REVOLUTION

BREAKING FREE

SAMANTHA MINERVA

"I AM NOT A PRODUCT OF MY CIRCUMSTANCES.
I AM A PRODUCT OF MY DECISIONS."

-STEPHEN COVEY

AMELIA & HAILEY-
ALL OF THIS IS FOR YOU

307.

Why am I still clinging
To this yucky toxic shit
The pieces of my past
I just won't let myself forget
Could it be it just feels comfortable
Like a numbing hazy drug
I can see how it's preferable
To pulling out that rug
The one that lies beneath my feet
Propping up my I
It'll be so bittersweet
To finally say goodbye
To the person I've created
To get me through this life
The truth is she's no longer needed
Cuz my Spirit is Alive

308.

There's a rage that lives inside of me
No one would ever know
I'd like to send it on its way
But it's got no place to go
This rage in me is justified
It shoulders all alone
The parts of me that weren't allowed
To be seen or held or known

309.

I'm trying to remember
Who I was as a girl
Before being taught
To hide away my pearl
I know I was hopeful
And always let down
Everything I believed in
Left me standing like a clown
How did I get here
Alone and afraid
Depending on others
Yet hating them the same
Am I still stuck
As that girl that was me?
Is there something I'm missing?
Something I can't see?
Maybe after all,
I can depend on me
Maybe that's what life has
Been forging into me
Self-sufficiency
A real sense of worth
Maybe that's the whole point of
My experience here on Earth

310.

Maybe I'm not me at all
Maybe I'm more than a name
Maybe life's supposed to be fun
Maybe it's all a big game
Maybe I'm not the only one
That struggles with burdens of flight
Maybe we're here to trudge through the darkness
To find that invincible Light

311.

Who the Hell let you
Dictate my value
Oh, that's right, I did
When I built my life around you
A house built on stilts
Submerged into sand
A shaky foundation
That was never meant to stand
The illusion of another
Is never secure
It is only within
That we can be sure
Once I found my true value
Outside of your perception
You could no longer hurt me
Cuz you're still my reflection

312.

I'm ready to heal
To jump off of this wheel
I'm ready to remember what it feels like
To feel
I'm ready to run
To jump and to skip
I've already set sail
Aboard this new ship
No more drama
No more strife
No more staying up at night
I choose to live
In peace and flow
I choose to Love
I choose to Grow

313.

Dear Me,
I will no longer accept
Being ignored
Being pushed aside
Being silenced
Being dimmed or hushed
I Am
Worthy of being seen deeply
Of being heard deeply
Felt deeply
Understood deeply
I Am
Worthy of being safe
Of being protected
Of being comfortable
I Am
Worthy of being confident
Of being beautiful and bold
Of being sensual and sexual
I Am
Worthy of being touched
Of being loved of being held
I Am
Worthy of being vulnerable
Of sharing how I feel
Of being listened to
I Am
Worthy of gentleness
Of care and softness
Of lightness and ease

I Am
Worthy of happiness
Of harmony and peace
Of stillness and silence
I Am
Worthy of abundance
Of joy and friendship
Of fun and laughter
I Am
Worthy of luxury
Of a beautiful home
Of a thriving community
I Am
Worthy of a stable secure happy healthy harmonious family
I Am
Worthy of an incredible life

314.

There's a fearlessness inside of me
I earned all on my own
I marched right into the abyss
And made the darkness known
I faced the deepest parts of me
Without batting an eye
Now I can finally say for sure
I'm not afraid to die
Cuz death surrounds us constantly
It's just a change of form
It's futile to fight this flow
There is no need to mourn
With death comes birth
With old comes new
Don't let your mind get blue
Once you're done with this here form
You'll start again brand new

315.

Love feels sticky
Icky
Full of obligations and strife
It feels like bitter resentment
And hiding all the knives
But love is not attachment
And I thought they were the same
I never could
Distinguish the two
Until I grew tired of the game
The game of lack
That we call love
The constant tug of war
Between the parts that know true love
And the parts always greedy for more

316.

I don't want to be attached
To need somebody else
I want to love
As openly
As the sky itself
I wish to have companions
And maybe a lover, too
But I don't want to be needed by them
Or to be stuck to them like glue
I wish to love myself
To thrive all on my own
Then I can meet a worthy King
To join me on my Throne

317.

Why am I scared of betrayal
Why does it hurt me so much
Is it because I betrayed me first
One could argue I betrayed me the worst
When I cut off my voice
To get you to love me
When I put on the makeup
So I wouldn't feel ugly
When I bought those new clothes
To make them accept me
When I caved on my No's
Catered to everyone except me
Come to think of it,
Where's Me in all this?
All I feel is darkness, restriction,
Unconscious blindness
When is the part
Where I stand for my heart?
When I take all the pain,
And turn it into Art?

318.

We see it all around us
It's everywhere we look
Folks searching for their "other"
As if that gets them off the hook
Don't get me wrong
I did it too
I gave all that I had
To try to be the perfect girl
The one he had to have
My search ran deep
I needed perfection
I wouldn't just settle
For passive affection
And thank God for this
Cuz I may had settled
For a love half true and gravely muddled
The only one to quench my thirst
Hid behind who I tried so hard to be
The person I'd been looking for
All along had always been
Me

319.

What do you do
When you run out of words
To express what lies deep in your soul
How can I say something
3 million ways
And still not get down to the core
There's a Truth that burns inside of me
So brightly I'm not sure it's mine
The Love that it shares
The wisdom it speaks
Makes it clear it must be
Divine
To get this out on paper
From a dictionary so hardly of use
Is like trying to nail down pure vapor
It's a task that requires a truce
A deal between spirit and man
To both play their own sacred part
To show up in sync
Put aside what they think
And pour forth their love
Straight from the Heart

320.

I'm terrified
To live with you
I can't escape this terror
The thought of it
Makes me clench
Anticipating error
I don't want to fight
Or suffocate
I yearn for harmony
I must release
This internal war
That wages within me

321.

I switched my state
From go to flow
Turned off my need to
Always know
I found a stillness
Deep within
After I climbed
That last mountain
I became we
And we became all
Suddenly I felt so small
Up upon that mountain's peak
I finally learned
The meaning of meek

322.

I clung so tightly onto me
Onto this old identity
I thought that I could move along
But I had never
Been so wrong
Me liked to fight
Me wanted to win
Me was not real
Me was just skin
Me screamed and cried
Me sobbed and moaned
As it crumbled
Off it's throne
Me put up quite a lofty fight
It had some nerve
It believed it was right
But finally
Me took a bow
Accepted defeat
I'll tell you how
Cuz Light came in
And made me see
That all there really is
Is We

323.

I've been holding tight
To the belief
That something bad's gonna
Happen to me
I did not know this was the case
Cuz outwardly
I was saving face
But deep inside grew seeds of doubt
Preventing things from ever working out
When you expect
To be abandoned
It's hard to shift
To reimagine
A future where
That's not the case
A real foundation
A solid place
As a kid we did not stay for long
Before a bulldozer came along
To knock away what we had built
So I learned to live on stilts
But this has been a hidden blessing
Cuz it's taught me to stop guessing
To stop building on fickle sand
And place my faith where I can firmly stand

324.

Family sticks together
Yet you always split us up
You'd rather just be comfortable
Than own up to your stuff
You'd rather run and hide away
Than stand up for your family
You'd rather be a lowly coward
And expect an amnesty
You are a spineless, ugly man
Undeserving of your fate
You let us down
You useless clown
And you deserve our hate

325.

I am a sinking clammy shrub
Shriveling in the cold

326.

You put me in the middle
As if I were old enough to hold
The massive tension
Between you two
That sure was mighty bold
Be a man!
Be a woman!
Speak up for your damn selves!
Don't put that garbage on your kids
As if their shoulders were shelves
We should not have to speak for you
That should be obvious
It's not our fault
Your relationship is
So disharmonious
So stand up tall
Grow some balls
And some goddamn restraint
To treat each other with respect
Not vile seething hate
If not for you
At least for us
The innocent in the middle
Cuz we can feel
So deeply how
You play us like a fiddle

327.

You hide in plain sight
Hold a veil over my eyes
You drown out my light
Keep me wrapped tight
You are my blindside
Beneath you I hide
You are clever and snide
Adept at keeping me tied
You give yourself away
In the guise of another
Most notably in
Your disguise as my lover
But I'm right on your tail
Getting closer by the day
It won't be long before
Your head I slay
You are my deepest shadow
My very first defender
But I need you no more
It'd be wise to surrender
A big thanks for your service
And good luck on your way
I have a life to build
And you're getting in my way

328.

The highs are so high
The lows are so low
I'd just like to rest in between
Not totally detached
Not completely enmeshed
Let's calculate both and find the mean
The middle way is the stillness
That watches with delight
It sees that huge win
And also that big fight
It's unshakable peace
In the eye of the storm
It's all-encompassing bliss
It has no dense form
The middle way is the Tao
It's the Buddha
The Christ
It's the Holy Trinity
The impurities sacrificed
This path is accessible
To every human being
It is what you have been seeking
It is altogether freeing

329.

Here I am again
Sinking into this dark space
I can feel the walls closing in
The hand covering my face
Why do I do this to me
Why do I let me get here
Surrounded by chaos
Clouded by fear
My mind's playing tricks
I know it to be
Cuz when I close my eyes
I'm still up there flying
What's down here for me
What do I still need to learn
Or maybe that's my choice now
To make a different turn
To lift myself up
From the ashes and muck
To take off the blindfold
Realize I've never been stuck
It's only been me
In this place I can't see
Perhaps I'm discovering
How to set myself free

330.

There's a beam in my chest
Both heavy and light
It's made of pure stardust
It's awesome and bright
It comes from the sky
Right in through my head
My connection to God
It transforms my lead
It's been leaking out sideways
And spurting out of cracks
Most of it is lost through
The hole in my back
An old stab wound, my first
When my innocence was stolen
Holding on to this pain
Is what keeps the hole open
I want to let go
But it's so hard to see
I completely forget it
Till my mirror confronts me
My lover, that is
He always reminds me
He doesn't do it on purpose
He just sees what's behind me
And I'm thankful for this
Or at least one day I'll be
Cuz if I don't patch up these holes
I'll never be free

331.

I want to surrender
I wish to be free
I'm digging to find
What blocks my release
Could it be anger
Resentment or blame?
Perhaps it is sorrow
Disappointment or shame
Whatever I'm holding
I wish to let go
But if I cannot see it,
How can I know?
The hard part about healing,
And most confusing, by far,
Is that we need others
To show us who we are
So when that monster shows up
In the form of another
Set aside your blame
And venture to discover
The key that they hold
The link that you need
To face your dark past
And excavate that seed

332.

Monsters and goblins
Demons and ghosts
Are they outside us?
Or are we their hosts?
If there's one thing I know
About what lurks in the dark
It's if we can see it,
It is in our own hearts
The difference between
Demons and angels
Is simply the lighting,
A shadow, an angle
In light of the Truth
They are but the same
Your difference in view
Determines the frame
Shine light in the dark
And what do you see?
What you thought was a monster
Was really just me

333.

What else can I say
That I've not already said
Why am I still searching
Still scratching my head
Where's the missing piece
In the puzzle of my life
Shall I keep venturing further,
Keep rolling the dice?
I'm afraid I can't choose
Cuz something compels me
Some force deep inside me
Something I cannot see
It yearns for the Truth
For bare naked reality
It won't settle for filters
For a skewed mentality
It penetrates personality
Sees past duality
It's on the hunt for clarity
For pure singularity

334.

You were never there for me
The way I needed you to be
You obliterated my innocence
Without any consequence
You crumpled up my clean slate
With all of your hate
Your hurt and your pain
Became tethered to my name
You were dominant and cruel
Took me for a fool
You did what you wanted
And fed me my gruel
I learned people were scary
And greedy and desperate
I had no one to turn to
No role model separate
I assumed your identity
To protect my own sanity
I adopted your mask
And you didn't have to ask
Just your sheer presence
And violent unpredictability
Are what built my armor
My impenetrability
But I've suffered enough
And so have my others
I'm breaking the chains
Reclaiming my udders
No more for you!
Or anyone like you!

I belong to me!
I am wild and free!
I have built my own safety
From my own inner well
And no one on this Earth
Could drag me back down to Hell

335.

What do I do now
How do I love
How do I open
How do I trust
I am solid and strong
I've fortified my castle
I trudged through the wreckage
I'm over that hassle
But I'm also alone
Has anything changed?
Are my boundaries too strong?
What's the point of this brigade

336.

Lower your voice
Do not talk to me that way
I am worthy of respect
And of having a say
Sit the fuck down
Do not come in here stomping
I will not take your mocking
I can see your rage chomping
Control yourself now
Or leave here at once
Work through your trauma
Cuz you're acting like a dunce
Who the hell gave you
Permission to spew
Your internal dumpster
On my heart that's brand new?
I am not just a girl
I'm a Princess of the Light
And I'm worthy of a father
Not a punk who needs to fight
Adjust your sight!
Think about me!
Is this really the man
You intended to be?
I'm supposed to be free
I am worthy of joy
I need a container
Not a little boy

337.

I'm ready to see you
For what you really are
Give it your best
You ain't getting far
I'm over your games
Your bondage has dissipated
I'm basking in sunlight
Illusion obliterated
You're welcome to test me
This very last time
If I get stressed
I'll just write a rhyme
I will not falter
I will stand strong
Confident in me
In who I know myself to be
Able to move now
Unshackled and free

338.

I can't say I'm not scared
That would be a lie
At best I am worried
Of things going awry
But I will stand strong
In the midst of this battle
I'm retiring my horse
Forfeiting the old saddle
I'm finding my strength
And my deepest reserves
To overcome this challenge
To settle my nerves
I'm ready to conquer
The pain that's plagued me
I'm ready to see now
The Truth about Me

339.

I was your pet
Your little girl
You showed me off
To all the world
You punctured me
In many ways
Then drank my blood
All of my days
I was afraid
I was alone
But I had no choice
Lest I be disowned
Or worse, destroyed
Like all your others
So I offered
My precious udders
You drank and drank
Till you had your fill
My love and light
Were in your gill
So this is how
I learned to love
To give and give
From an empty cup
I do this to
Protect my self
To ensure my safety
Though it hurts like hell

340.

Where'd I go
Where's little me
I'm trapped somewhere
I cannot see
I gave and gave
The best of me
Now what is left
For me to be?

341.

I sure do hope
It's not too late
To patch up these holes
Rewrite my fate
My story was
I have no worth
But I'm planning now
A whole rebirth
A brand new me
Though not new at all
The me I was
When I learned to crawl
The me that sees
Through innocent eyes
The me that was
Before the lies
Who was I then
That little girl
I loved to dance
To sing and twirl
That me was free
A pure clean slate
That me knew nothing
Of pain or hate
I call you now
To come forth
To rise up
From the earth
I've done the work
You're safe to play

You're free to dance
To have fun all day
You're safe to be
To live in the Now
You're safe to love
Please remind me how

342.

Get your dirty hands off her
That precious little girl
Go clean up your act
Stop feeding on her pearl

343.

The battle in my head
Is coming to a head
I'm no longer dead
No longer wish I was dead
The defenses are down
Each side is emerging
Noticing each other
And the inevitable converging
Each side is confused
Thought it was being used
Thought it was being attacked
Tormented, abused
Each side saw the other
Reflected without
It saw its own fear
Limitation and doubt
But standing here now
Defenseless and naked
Only Truth remains-
This merging was fated

344.

I'm angry for reasons
Too deep to discover
The memories are stored
As feelings undercover
My mind cannot help
On this quest any further
My body holds the answers
And it's time that I heard her

345.

I'm letting all go now
Falling into surrender
I don't know what I'll find
But anything's better
Than being a pretender
I'm sinking into stillness
Releasing the reigns
Focusing on love
I'm done with the games
My own beauty surrounds me
The Earth
She abounds me
Rainbows all around me
Sunshine's finally found me

346.

I'm done with the distractions
The sharp mental chatter
The click clack of the keyboard
The total mind scatter
What's this thing in my head
And how do I use it
It seems all I've learned
Is how to abuse it
I force it to do things
And it forces me right back
This is not partnership
This is attack
This is competition
It's a war up in there
So I'm sinking down here
Where the warm coast is clear
My heart never lies
And she cannot deceive
It's a beautiful landing
A cozy reprieve
She welcomes me home
She knows what I need
And she's not even mad
For ignoring her heed
To let go of the chaos
The mental riff raff
Feels like coming in from the cold
Into a warm bath
The candles are lit
The jazz is a-playin'

I breathe nice and slow
My body gently swaying
And the deeper I sink
The more peaceful I feel
Only God knows why
I ever clutched to that wheel

347.

It's one thing to know
Quite another to do
What's the difference, you ask,
Between one and two?
Knowing is a candle
But action is the flame
You can have all the answers
But still must play the game
There's nothing to win
And there's even less to lose
What matters most of all
Is the attitude you choose

348.

I am an old sage
I've trekked in from afar
I've seen the whole world
I've grasped all the stars
I came for one thing
And that is to remind you
That everything you need
Is already inside you

349.

You see with your heart
Not with your eyes
And don't believe those eyes
You'll only see lies
The Truth never dies
It always lives inside
Should you choose to ignore
The thoughts behind which it resides

350.

I surrender to my heart
It knows what I want
Not what I think I need
Or what my memories flaunt
My heart is my compass
It knows my true North
It tugs my legs onward
And bathes me in warmth

351.

I finally found Reality
It was with me all along
It was underneath my pretenses
And ideas of right and wrong
It bobbed right up to the surface
When I just stopped holding it down
I did not have to travel far
Or even leave my town
I had to close the eyes upstairs
And use the ones within
All along my heart's been waiting
For her journey to begin

352.

Dangerously deep
Trapped by the tides
When I come up for air
I am slammed to the sides
I'm backed into a cave
I see no escape
The waves are'a fierce
In this punic hellscape
The weight of the water
Holds me under for long
The roar of the sea
Silences my song
The tentacles beneath
They grasp at my legs
They yearn to transform me
To gift me sea legs
But I fight against surrender
I'm gasping for air
I'm all alone in here
There's no one to care
Suddenly
There's a break
From the sharp pounding waves
Suddenly
An escape
Appears in the cave
And I'm faced with the choice
To emerge or let go
Emergence looks easy
But then I'd never know

What lies in the depths
That's been calling my name
I could go back to shore
But up there's all the same
I take one last breath
I relinquish this fight
I close my eyes gently
And I sink
Out of sight

353.

I don't want to think
I just want to be
I don't want confusion
I just want to see
I don't want to be fake
I just want to be me
I don't want a parade
I just want to be free

354.

What can I say
That has never been said?
Is there anything novel
Inside of my head?
What about my heart
Have we felt all the feelings?
Surely there's a way
To burst through these ceilings
Or maybe that's the point,
What keeps this show reeling
When we each play our part
In the grand scheme of dealings
As parts of a whole
We each have our niche
In the fabric of reality
Each human a stitch

355.

I would like to believe
That my life has a point
But I catch myself looking for
A way out of this joint
To where?
I don't know
And sometimes I don't care
Sometimes all I can think
Is that Life is unfair
But then I look at a flower
And I sense a grand plan
Who's to say that that flower
Don't belong in this clan?
Who's to say it's not perfect
Just right as it is
Who's to say I'm any different
In the life that I live

356.

What does it mean
To be alive?
Is there a reason
To thrive or to strive?
What are we doing here?
Why do we come?
Furthermore, why do we
Make ourselves numb?
If life is a journey,
Which I do believe so,
To where are we headed?
Where is there to go?
And what does it look like
When we finally arrive?
Is meaning inherent?
Or ours to derive?

357.

I surrender my identity
And all that I planned to be
I no longer cling to
The ideas that I've had of me
I give it all up
There is nothing I need
Use me for service
My vessel a steed
I relinquish desire
I forego ambition
I submit my human
To a state of submission
I take up my cross
My reason for being
I rest now in spirit
My true state of freedom

358.

I would rather cease living
Than to be a dreadful mother
I cannot bear the thought of
Shadow deeds undercover
If there's anything I'm missing
I beg you to show me
I'll do what I have to
To cut it all out of me

359.

I am trapped in a hall of mirrors
Thick fog surrounds
Which is me and
Which is you

360.

It seems I'd been waiting
So tragically long
For someone to tell me
That I do belong
I'd been searching for someone
To pick up my pieces
And squish them together
Till the fracturing ceases
I was seeking validation
My reason for being
I wanted someone to prove that
My life had some meaning
It took me so long
Before I could see
That the person I was searching for
Had always been Me
I needed Me to be there
To show Me the way
I needed Me to wrap Me up
When I had a hard day
It was my duty to discover
My place here on Earth
It was up to Me to determine
What I was worth
Once I took ownership
Of my role on this battleship
I became confident
And my joy became prominent
I no longer needed
Any external voice

After learning the hard way
My whole life
Was my choice

361.

I'm angry for reasons
Too deep to discover
The memories are stored
As feelings undercover
My mind cannot help
On this quest any further
It's time to give my body what she needs
Nurture

362.

Insecurity had plagued me
For as long as I could remember
I don't know where it came from
Or why it came with a temper
It was never mine to hold
But I chose it anyway
I suppose it felt more comfortable
To live in a powerless way
I suppose that I dimmed my own light
For fear of what others might say
I chose to live out of sight
On the fray in a world full of gray
I stayed hidden to keep myself safe
From vultures searching for prey
I was cloaked in bitter dismay
Too guarded to see another way
But as I cleared up the clutter
The baggage and debris
I'd collected all those years in the dark,
The Truth became evident
The World could not benefit
From me hiding my God-given
Spark

363.

The world is so bland
Colorless and dull
When we have all these lenses
Attached to our skull
A filter of fear
Siphons out all the pink
Whenever we ask ourselves
"What might they think?"
The green turns to gray
When we go about our day
Oblivious to
What our heart wants to say
Blue turns to brown
When we repress that frown
And force ourselves to smile
Like a big circus clown
Let's talk about red
It wants others dead
But we can't have those feelings
So our red turns to dread
Worst of all, white,
Our true, shining light,
Gets muddled and puddled
In spite of this fight
Can't you see that the colors
They give our life meaning
Each feeling a tinge
A necessary gleaming
When we shut down our feelings
For the sake of conformity

We abandon our essence
We become a deformity
Your Life was designed
To be viewed in full color
If you let yourself feel
It'll clear up that ulcer
Take off that mask
And let yourself see
The full spectrum of Reality
You were destined to Be

364.

Mama!
My warmth
The only thing I've known
You've left me in this crib
To cry all on my own
Don't you know I need you?
Isn't that easy to tell?
What did I do to deserve this?
To be left all alone here in Hell

365.

I'm done trying to fix you
To change you
To make you see
The reality of what
You are doing to me
The breadcrumbs you give
Of love and affection
No longer suffice
You've lost my attention
I deserve more
Than half-hearted effort
I deserve presence
And cashmere and velvet
I accepted less
Cuz it's what I was taught
It's all I was worth
I was taught as a tot
But the reality that I
Was too dependent to see
Is that even back then
He did not deserve me
I never lost hope
That I'd fix him one day
That if I could be perfect
Then maybe he'd stay
And give me the love
That I wanted so bad
The love that I needed
That only he had
But he never did change

Never once came around
He still offers morsels
But I'm no longer spellbound
I see that his lack
Inability to give
Is a reflection of him
Not of something I did
And so therefore you
Are too off the hook
You have a nice life
I'm writing a new book
In my book I receive
All the love that I give
I find a real man
Goodbye, little kid

366.

I found my worth
Right where I had left it
In the hands of a man
Who did not deserve it
I gave of my love
My devotion and time
I gave ceaselessly
With no reason or rhyme
You took and you took
You hoarded and held
You rarely gave back
True affection withheld
But who's to blame here?
I now see it is me
If I'm the one giving,
How can I blame he?
Once upon a time
My true worth was forgotten
But at this point in time
That memory is rotten
So I choose to let go
To forgive those who couldn't see
My heart and my worth
And all that I would be
If anyone can't see my worth now
At least it won't be me

367.

Once I learned to take responsibility
For everything that I see
No longer did my mind
Have control over me
I could see through its tactics
Of projection and blame
And realize the culprit;
Me deflecting my shame
I was playing a game
That cannot be won
It can only be risen above
Fully overstood
The mind is amazing,
Now don't get me wrong,
But it is just a tool
We program the song
But it's our choice to make
There's no such thing as fate
Just childhood software
That you need to update
So the next thing you see
Stop and ask yourself why
Your limited view
Keeps you from the sky

368.

A dead crow on my step
Cawing my name
He came to remind me
We're not all the same
At large, we are one
But on Earth, one is many
He reminded me I am surrounded
By plenty
He urged me to caw
Whilst the clock was still ticking
He lay there to prove
There was no time for clipping
The wings of my Soul
Who came for a purpose
Who came to rise up
Out of the circus
He came to transform me
To gift me my wings
He came to assure me
The World needs me to sing

369.

Every life
A masterpiece
From snails to frogs to doves
Each blade of grass
A vital piece
Of everything
That makes up
Love

370.

I asked to be transported up
To where the Gods do dwell
I met with a voice
Who gave me a choice
To rise
Or keep living in Hell
Of course, I chose the former
But as a hardened performer
Hell was not easy to tell
My picture of paradise
Required a sacrifice;
Everything I thought that I knew
Initiated into stillness
Guided into realness
The Truth slowly came into view
The God's are not out there
The God's are all right here
They exist inside of me
And in you

371.

That's the thing about time
It can change on a dime
Any moment you can be someone new
There's a trick to this, though
It requires insight, you know
Into why you do the things that you do
This insight is brutal
It's honest
It's raw
And it will take some time
For those layers to thaw
But once at the center
The heart of your being
You'll realize the magnitude
Of what you weren't seeing
You'll see your true essence
In front of your face
And recognize the lies
That were taking its place
The Truth will be clear
That the lies were just fear
That the voices you hear
You should have never held dear
Cuz reality's a brick
It's attached to your face
The only thing you need
To see it

Is grace
And then time disappears
You can be what you are
And you'll remember what that is;
A wandering Star

372.

We spend our whole lives
Believing we're a half
Till the day that we die
Then we have a big laugh
Not only are we whole
(There's no halves of a soul)
We are more than capable
Of carrying on alone
If we choose to partake
In the dance of a mate
It is vital we know this
Before it's too late
If you think that your partner
Gives you something you lack,
If you depend on one person
To always have your back,
If you try to use another
To fill up your heart,
It will always lead to heartache
It will tear you apart
Cuz Truth will carry on
Whether you see it or not
The fairytales of love
Are just lies we've been taught

373.

Dear younger me
I'm sorry I did not see
The pain that I was causing you
Just trying to feel free
Dear younger me
I'm sorry I didn't have your back
When I let them take your innocence
And hung your heart on a rack
Dear younger me
I'm sorry for not seeing your worth
Instead, I believed in the lies I was taught
About being defective from birth
Dear younger me
I'm sorry for hanging you out to dry
When I silenced your feelings
With gallons of beer
And didn't allow you to cry
Dear younger me
I'm sorry for leaving you cold
For making amends
With harmful fake friends
Instead of taking your hand to hold
Dear younger me
Thank you for forgiving me
I'll never leave you again
Now that I can see

374.

Thank you for coming on down here
Choosing to participate
In the masterpiece of my life
My rising up out of self-hate
Without your loving neglect
And carefully planned manipulation
I could not have earned my degree
In rapid regeneration
Your inadequate administration
Of proper parental accommodation
Has provided perfect catapultation
For master manifestation
And I thank my foes
Cuz God only knows
I would have gotten no where
Without you
The betrayals you forayed
Within this masquerade
Truly set the stage
For my honorary placade
My trials my tears
My fires my fears
I thank you all for coming
You've played your roles perfectly
Extraordinarily earnestly
You've made me
Who I am today

375.

The curtain has dropped
The Oz has been seen
I can finally see
What everything has meaned
I've been playing a part
A role with a mask
Life's a beautiful art
A simple complex task
Each one of us here
We know what we're doing
We pretend to forget
To keep ourselves musing
It's fun, don't ya think
To live right on the brink
Of reality and illusion
Clarity and confusion
To be dropped into place
On this liquid time-space
And experience interspace
And experience true grace
I don't know about you
But my time's been a blast
I can finally look back and
Appreciate my past

376.

Everything I learned
About love was fucked up
I learned it was scary
Destructive
Abrupt
I mistook intensity for love
When it is nothing but
I confused romance
And slow dance
For a warm flowing cup
I believed passion
And yelling
Anger and fighting
Were proof of a bond
That was worth defending
But love needs no proof
It just simply is
Love has no boundaries
It's beyond hers and his
Love's all around us
It's in everything we see
But I just could not feel it
Cuz I distorted it
With We

377.

I'm done with the pretending
Avoiding the inevitable ending
Hoping for a change
Playing the rigged game
There's no way to win
Cuz it's all an illusion
A mirage in the desert
A wasted quest for fusion
I could have lived a normal life
Worked a normal job
Been a normal wife
But an impulse inside would not let me be
Cuz an impulse from above needed me to see
The love that's within me
That never runs out
The love that's elusive
When I'm looking without
And the closer I got
The more painful it felt
To let go of the safety
Of my useless seat belt
I was clutching so hard
To my need for another
Which really only was
Unworthiness undercover
It was keeping me blind
Dependent and fractured
It was eating at my mind

A crisis manufactured
And I finally had enough
I grew weary of the fight
I finally surrendered
To the Truth of my own Light

378.

I tried to skip all the steps
Of filling my own cup
I thought it'd be easier
If I let you fill it up
But a series of hiccups
Many right after another
Forced me to wake up
From my deep, dreadful slumber
The teacher was in
My excuses were out
I could no longer settle
No longer sell out
It was high time for me
To be schooled in self-love
What felt like a curse
Was a gift from Above
Cuz only through the pain
Was my neediness revealed
Years of striving in vain
Allowed those layers to be peeled
Right down to my core
The day I said no more
And stood for myself
Dependency falling to the floor

379.

Dear little me
I hear you
I see you
I feel you
I am you
Teach me how to know you
Remind me how to love
Show me what you need
Tell me when you need a hug
I am here
I am present
I want to be your rock
Whisper me the codes
To open up your lock
I want to be your landing
Where you're comfortable to be
I vow to keep you safe
So that you can run free
I'll never leave your side
I'll always have your back
I'll never let you believe again
That there's anything you lack
I'll give you all the love
You've searched for all your life
I'll wrap you up in peace
And block out all the strife
Dear little me
It's safe to come out from hiding
I'm done with all the violence,
The yelling and the fighting

Please put your hand in mine
Let's do this thing together
I'll be the container for your heart
So it can stay light as a feather

380.

What I searched for in you
Was in me all along
What I heard in your voice
Was an echo of my song
The love that I saw
In the depths of your eyes
Was my very own essence
Wrapped in disguise

381.

I'm cutting the cord
I won't take any more
Of your bastardized "love"
See yourself to the door
I know what I'm worth
And I know who I am
I have nothing to prove
And nothing to win
Things have never been well
Between us, it's always been Hell
You have never had my back
Emotions stuck in a well
I am letting you go
Now my mind is at ease
I held on way too long
Afraid of this release
Afraid to stand on my own
Afraid to pick up my life
I was building on sand
While you sharpened your knives
Always ready to cut me
Real deep in the back
Whenever I got my bearings
You'd stage another attack
I could never be safe
In your cold lifeless arms
You have never protected me
You've only caused harm
I'm not looking for completion
Cuz I am whole myself

But I will find a partner
With whom I can build shelves
Together for our home
Filled with peace and prosperity
We will create a sanctuary
A reprieve full of harmony
And you are not welcome
You are left in the cold
Hopefully you learn your lessons
Before you get old

382.

What does loyalty
Mean to me
I'm not sure anymore
Don't know what to believe
I gave you my love
Everything that I had
To build up a lie
That ended so bad
Everything that I knew
Crumbled with you
In whom I put my hope
To just be left blue
You tore out my heart
You ate it for dinner
Then you asked for desert
Something a bit thinner
So I poured out my blood
I wrang myself dry
All of this just for you
To still say goodbye
You left me with nothing
Turned hope to despair
Is this all life is?
It doesn't seem fair
I don't know how to give me
The love that I need
I don't know how to forgive
Your sick, ruthless greed
Worst of all
I can't figure

How to release all this shame
As if somehow, for all of this,
I am to blame
So here I sit
Motionless
Stuck with your name
Trying like hell
To reclaim my Flame

383.

My perception changed
When I changed
People stayed the same
But no longer looked the same
No longer treated me the same
No longer sounded the same
I was in a new game
Transported in time
To a place life made sense
Every lesson a rhyme

384.

There is no such thing as chance
In this life
It's all a dance
Choreographed by our souls
Who witness our trance

385.

I tried to appease you
Always wanted to please you
Too timid and shy to rock the boat
I wanted your love
Became the white dove
Flying back and forth over your moat
I flew over for crumbs
Scraps of affection
And your crocodile offered me
A false sense of protection
But I grew weary one day
So, I perched by a lake
Finally noticing
How much you would take
And how little you'd give-
Just the flecks from your sieve
You were no messiah
Just a simple pariah
Too selfish to accept any blame
But the tables have turned
Now that I have learned
That I can simply fly away from this game

386.

I looked for you
And what did I see
In the shattered mirror
Just pieces of me
I searched for love
And what did I find
But solitary stillness
Just outside my mind
I sought for Truth
And what was uncovered
The answer to every question
I had ever wondered
I asked for a sign
And what did I get
The truth about me
In everyone that I met

387.

Way, way up high
Above land, in the sky
Lies a bird's eye view
Inaccessible to your eyes
It is guarded by veils
Of ignorance and lack
It is hidden in plain sight
Once you're brave enough to ask
The deeper questions of life,
Once you're tired of the strife
Ready to lay down that knife
And reclaim your Life

388.

I surrender I surrender
I surrender I surrender
I surrender I surrender
I surrender I surrender
I surrender I surrender
I surrender I surrender
I surrender I surrender
I surrender I surrender
I surrender I surrender
I surrender I surrender
I surrender I surrender
I surrender I surrender
I surrender I surrender
I surrender I surrender
I surrender I surrender

389.

Falling falling falling
Deep into
My Soul
Sensing the power
Relinquishing control
Taking my stand
Once and for all
Which is really just a fall
Not a stand at all
As I fall,
I rise up
I'm greeted by my King
He was always there
Hidden beneath my wings
My light and dark have balanced
My face been touched by Grace
I smile at the sunlight,
And welcome Death's embrace

390.

There's a plan for your life
A river, if you will
It flows along just swimmingly
If only you sit still
The more we try to poke and prod
And steer the ship ourselves
The more it takes
To hear our God
Telling us to
Just be ourselves

391.

I ain't writing to please
Spent long enough on my knees
I am writing to communicate
Soul to soul
If a poem upsets you
It's the part that protects you
It's the anger that has got
No place to go
So don't get mad at me
Instead stop and see
When and where that rage
Was born
Long ago

392.

I'm a gardener,
Of sorts,
I dig and dig for pain
And when I've dug around enough
I stop and feel the rain
I till for treasures
Long lost gems
Feelings of sadness and shame
I water them with seeds of hope
Then play the waiting game
Up they sprout
In my tender care
Flourishing
Nourishing
Beautifully bare
I dig up the darkness
And bring it to light
I do this because
It enhances my sight

393.

All around me
Fires flare
This heat consumes my soul
It burns the things
I thought I knew
So that I may be whole
I used to run,
Prevent the sweat,
But now I lie and wait
Cuz I've learned that once the heat is done
I pass another gate

394.

Here I lie
Upon my cross
I've chosen it
To bear
No longer scared of it
No longer running
No longer hiding
I know how much
Upon this is riding
I bid my time
I had my fun
I heard my call
My life begun

395.

I am a Leader
I go where most fear to tread
I am a Leader
Countless times I've been back from the dead
I am a Leader
I write my own tune
I am a Leader
I pave a path out of the ruin

396.

You're a monster in disguise
I can see it in your eyes
Shape-shifting, conniving
Your dark side is thriving
You're ugly and despicable
Overwhelming and predictable
No more!!!!!!!! I say!!!
Stay the fuck away from me!
I let myself be stuck like glue
Because it's all I ever knew
But I'm breaking free
Reclaiming me
My heart and my authority

397.

I've seen the world
Through your filthy lens
For thirty years
Today it ends
Your passive aggression
Demon possession
Victim consciousness
Had left me stifled
Unjustly bridled
Deep in my subconsciousness
Miserable bitch
Self-serving witch
You kept me tethered
Enmeshed in the death ward
Stuck like a fly to a trap
I've taken responsibility
For all of the things you refused to see
And wore your secrets like a mask
But it wasn't even me
My true personality
Buried
Because you never thought to ask

398.

The war in my head
Has come to a halt
Now that I've realized
Who's really at fault
The ghosts of my past
AKA mom and dad
Had conditioned my mind
Undermined my launchpad
I was trapped with their thoughts
Assigned to their battles
I was strapped with the task
Of cleaning up their shambles
And I trudged through it all
Like a good little soldier
Never once taking note of them
Breathing over my shoulder
I made it through to the Sun
With medals of honor
Blood stains on my face
Bullet wounds in my armor
Any the irony is
Though I served with all my might
This wasn't even my battle
It was never mine to fight

399.

Hello, old friend
So nice to see you
I've missed you more than words can say
Goodbye, old friend
We've come to the end
I've waited so long for this day

400.

You wonder why you're miserable
Even though your life looks great
You start to think that possibly
This may just be your fate
But let me tell you something
You already know deep inside
The reason that you're unfulfilled
Is cuz society lied
They lied about your college degree
They lied about your job
They lied about your perfect wedding
To that perfect guy named Bob
They lied about where knowledge comes from
And sold you the wrong books
They replaced your kids with dogs and said
Just focus on your looks
No matter where these lies came from
You're the one that took the bait
It's why you scroll for hours
And can't escape that deep self-hate
The Truth is there's a gaping hole
Deep inside your chest
And as long as you ignore its calls
It will not let you rest
You can stuff it full of food
And vodka over ice
You can fly it to the moon

But none of it will suffice
The only thing that fills this hole
Is presence from within
So take a breath and close your eyes
It's the perfect time to begin

401.

There's a starving girl inside of me
She dwells somewhere I cannot see
I feed her scraps from time to time
Of my affection, love and time
She screams for chocolate, cookies, cake
Unluckily for her, I do not bake
She forces me to eat those chips
Because it's all that she can get
It's the only comfort that she knows
A full belly feels better than being alone
Of course my body craves real food
It would certainly enhance my mood
But the food I choose is mirroring
The type of love I give to me
Now that I've finally stopped to listen,
To hear the truth that I've been missin'
I know exactly what she needs
And so it's time to plant those seeds

402.

I'm floating around
In this liminal space
Not knowing my place
Just saving face
I'm waiting for something
Though what, I'm not sure
My mind is all fuzzy
My world is a blur
Time has stopped
For a time
Though it feels like forever
Suspended in place
Ever since my surrender
I'm not a pretender
Or am I?
Who knows?
Where's the piece that I need
To bring this puzzle to close?
I can feel the Truth coming
My only option is to wait
I've done all I could do
The rest is up to Fate

403.

My body is tingly
It speaks in pure form
I can hear it so clearly
Since I no longer perform
No longer play a role
No longer wear that mask
I became unbelievably sensitive
Since I threw away that flask
The numbness has subsided
The emotions were invited
To surface once again
So I could feel
I used to feel so cold
But now my bones are thawing
I might have stayed that way
If it wasn't for the gnawing
The gnawing and the knowing
That there must be something deeper
The gnawing and the knowing
That life should be much sweeter
Not hard
Or clammy
Rigid
Or brambly
But soft
And flowing
Slow

And glowing
And it is, I discovered,
Once I let myself feel it
Once I stopped being afraid
Once my heart let me heal it

404.

I am at peace
The war has subsided
Only because
It's what I've decided
Each side has surrendered
Glimpsed the big picture
Intertwining together
A beautiful mixture
The left and the right
The light and the dark
Daytime and night
The flow and the spark
I am one
I am whole
I am utterly complete
The clutter's been cleared
My temple is neat

405.

No matter what I do
I can't seem to get ahead
I try and try and strive and strive
Yet still just want to curl up in bed
I'm climbing a mountain
With ten thousand bricks
Stacked quite neatly upon my back
And all that I have
Are the promises of victory
Tucked away in my nap sack
To where am I going
I haven't a clue
I have a broad vision
An idea or two
And what keeps me going
Yes, what is the point
I'll never find out
If I reach my breakpoint
Or perhaps that's the point
But then I try to surrender
And still I'm restricted
Trapped here forever
I just want to cry
Breakdown for a day
But I don't have that choice
I have dragons to slay
And why am I fighting
And who am I defending
This whole entire show
Just feels like pretending

Like a big, funny joke
Or at least it should be
And who's the butt of this joke
Well, I guess
That'd be me

406.

At last!
I am free!
I've made my way back
To me
I can run, jump and play
I don't care what others say!
I found my resistance
My identification with assistance
My defensive persistence
It was all just such a hindrance
I stepped out of my role
That rigid personality
The multitude of protectors
The suffocating familiarity
I let it all go
Cuz none of it was me
It took living with my parents
For me to finally see
The layers I created
To shield the original me
It took peeling back each layer
And following my glee
To get to where I am now
Naked and ecstatic
Free from all the burdens
In that filthy dusty attic
Forgiveness became easy
Only once I saw
That my parents weren't my parents
No no, not at all

I was raised by other pretenders
Defenders playing a role
Whose inner children were also lost
Trapped inside a hole
And then that's when I learned the Truth
The secret of us all
We're all just searching for a way
To be who we were when we were small

407.

Who gave you permission
To pick at my brain
To poison my thoughts
To make me so vain
I guess these are my lessons
Upon this time space
To take back my mind
To accept Love's grace

408.

Thump
A small sign of affection from you
And I jump
My heart skips a beat
And I leap to protect it
An instant defeat
Of any possible connection
I won't let it feel
I forbid it to hope
I can't take the risk
That it falls down that slope
I know it wants to open
But I can't let it open for you
Because of our past
And the things that you do
Or rather, what you don't
What I learned not to expect
Like simply checking in,
A basic hello text
My disappointment did not begin with you
But you sure portray it well
If I didn't know the Truth
It'd sure be difficult to tell
And, it was, for many years
I stayed in that dark hole
Until I fought off the abyss
And discovered I am Whole
Until I faced the parts of me
That were stuck playing a role
Until I finally gained the courage

To peer within that keyhole
Until I realized you were a reflection
Never out to get me
Just a simple projection
Only then did I finally see
I could love you
Because now I loved me

409.

And now begins
The time I learn
Of how to give and take
The balance I've sought
All of my life
I'm fighting the urge to just flake
On this lesson
I am stressin'
I don't want to mess up this chance
I've learned how to give
Now must learn to receive
In order to complete this dance

410.

I gave and gave
And gave and gave
And gave and gave and gave
I had nothing to give
It was quite primitive
I thought I was just being brave
It was nearly impossible
To pull back my power
It felt somehow wrong
It felt rather sour
And it hurt
Quite a bit
To finally admit
The pain I was causing
To me
It was ugly
To see
What I sunk down to be
To prop others up
From my knees
I didn't know how to stand
A fresh baby doe
Just finding my bearings
Thrown into a rodeo
And whip after whip
Lash after lash
I had finally had enough
I'd been condensed to ash

It was time for my rise
And it took many tries
But I'd never go back
It would be my demise

411.

Stop resisting
Stop grasping
Stop clinging
Life will be
What it is
You're only fooling yourself
To think you have control over this
There's a power that lies
Just outside your grasp
When you align with your Self
That is our task

412.

Great Spirit
Wise Owl
I call on you now
Mother Nature
My creator
I count on you to show me how
To leave myself behind
To submerge into the masses
To see with your eyes of Love
To throw away my glasses
I yearn for wholeness
As I bask in peace
As the wants and desires
Of my I are released
What's left
In this stillness
A faint shining light
And as I sink deeper
More does it grow bright
Until
At last
Recognition occurs
The Light, it is I
The I without eyes
And the me, left behind
Just a fragment of time

413.

Aha!
Clarity
I can finally see
Yes, I've said that before,
But that was not the real me
This spiral keeps spinning
My mind keeps untwisting
Personality unraveling
Yet I'm not even traveling
Behind the multitude of masks
In the Sun, my soul has basked
It was only I who could not see
The perfect world in front of me
Because I fought for my suspension
I held on tightly to my tension
I clung to survival
An illusion of safety
But I gave it all up
To finally find me

414.

Shatter my I,
My perception of me
Let it all crumble
So the Truth I can see
I'm smashing the mirror
That keeps me imprisoned
Transcending beliefs
That keep me conditioned
I'm cranking down that drawbridge
Between head and heart
I'm harnessing the darkness
Crafting it into Art
I'm going back to the start
To the essence of me
I'm removing the blinders
I'm a horse running free
The wind at my back
And the wind is in me
I'm no longer bound
I'm free to just
Be

415.

The answer is Love
The question?
Who cares
Love's all around us
Love is the air
It's over here
It's over there
It's in my skin
It's in your hair
It's not a flair
It's not a fad
It's not something good and
It's not something bad
It's all of those things
And more
It's a never-ending stream
A wide-open door
Forevermore
Forevermore
It cannot be stored
Or grasped
Or gorged
It always is
And always was
It always will be
It lives in the bugs
And the birds and the trees
The waves of the ocean
It caresses your skin
As you rub on your lotion

It wraps you in warmth
As a hug from your kid
It carries on still
When you blow your lid
It's ever present
It cannot be lost
It can be ignored,
But at a steep cost
It can't be confined
Although you might try
To dwindle it down
To one girl and one guy
It accepts no illusions
It stands in spite of hate
You need no special key
To open up Love's gate
To simply let it in
Is all it really takes
To let it flow right through you
There is no time to wait

416.

To know yourself
Is to love yourself
And to love yourself
Is to skate
Down the slow lane of life
Doing 25
Free to be you
No need for a knife
Gentle and easy
Not sticky or cheesy
But graceful and breezy

417.

I've been a fighter
All my life
Skilled in combat
Battles rife
But I grew tired
Became weary
A soldier's life
Got quite dreary
I longed for love
I yearned for youth
When I could trust
The simple truth
Of what I saw
Before my eyes
Before the veils
Before the lies
I ache for sunlight
Glimmering hope
I'm done hanging
At the end of my rope
Naivety
Simplicity
Femininity
Divinity
I call upon you now
Remind me who I am
Nourish me with Love
Tell me,
Who is Sam

418.

I stand
And I say
No!
I will not let you in
You may not have
A single morsel
You cannot fool me with that grin
I see your eyes
Your moot disguise
I know just who you are
The energy
Attached to me
That tries to eat my star
You creep around
In different forms
I see your sneaky face
It's time for me
To stand my ground
And put you in your place

419.

Weighed down
By chains of gold
Voices shouting
You're too young!
Then
You're too old!
Who are these people
Who tell us what to be
What to think, what to know
What to love, to believe?
Buy this! Buy that!
Everyone needs a cat
10 sweaters for winter
Shoes to match every pant
You must possess these things
Work harder if you can't
But who's being possessed?
Is it you?
Or your things?
Underneath all that crap
You actually have wings
You can fly
Yes, it's true!
But right now, you're too heavy
Get rid of your knick knacks,
Your gadgets, your chevy
Drop your notions, your worries,
Expectations and pride
Forget what society taught you...
It lied

Money's just paper
Or worse, ones and zeros
It can't keep you safe
You are your own hero
Abundance is energy
It's ease and it's flow
If you tune into the rhythms
Of life, you will grow
On time and in peace
As it should be
So let go of your baggage
And set yourself
Free

420.

I've leaned on you
For far too long
Your peaceable
Helpless
Dependant
I thought I was safe
Being taken good care
But really
You were just a
Depressant
And it's not even you
It's a facet of me
A tightly bound ghost
From my past
That's kept me in chains
Holding my reigns
Preventing me from
Gaining a grasp
On myself
On my path
You keep me in a bloodbath
Instead of the place I belong
In a robe
On my throne
Completely unowned
Happy and singing my song
Fulfilled by reality
And my own immortality
Not getting along
To go along

I belong to the free
I am but a tree
I cannot be bound
I am limitless sound
I am hope
I am awe
I am natural and raw
I am here
I am now
And I do disallow
Any energy
To treat me any other way

421.

Yes
Let it flow
Let it come in
And go
I am back here
Observing it all
Sounds aren't for me
Because I can see
I dance in the wind
I am one with the Sea
I am wild
And gentle
I am deeper
Than mental
I live in your bones
If I speak
It's in moans
I am humble
And brave
Never been to
The grave
I am everything
And nothing
I'm a hummingbird
Buzzing
I am in you
And around you
Guaranteed to
Astound you
Once you see through

My eyes
Up here in
The skies
In the stillness of Truth
My secrets apparent
You and your life
Everything
Transparent

422.

I don't want to think
I just want to feel
I am already whole
I am already healed
I just want to be
I just want to see
I just want to float
I want to be free

423.

I'm preparing
For my birth
Of Spirit
To Earth
In a deep state of flow
Of surrender
Of trust
I'm releasing my grasp
Allowing the thrust
To propel me to Life
I am my own
Midwife
I am breathing
And humming
Heart gently pumping
I am swaying
And soothing
Mind softly musing
I am naked
And bare
Long flowing hair
Hunched in cocoon
Hands folded in prayer
Everything within me
Nothing out there

424.

Side A and side B
They never used to see
Eye to eye
They were always at war
But then A said to B
Let's involve C
C what we're doing this for
An outside perspective
No skin in the game
A reliable detective
No interest in blame
C came right around
And you know what he found
Both sides underground
Both sides were spellbound
They were on the same side
But they had not a clue
They wanted the same things
Though neither one knew
The dirt was too thick
The worms were too many
It was easier to hate
Albeit mighty deadly
So C said to A
Just chill for a day
Observe, and don't make a sound
A came to see
Maybe just maybe
He and B were actually bound
Two sides of a coin

Two arms of a man
His very own kin
From his very own clan
What surprised him the most
Was that he was a host
To some voices that were not his own
They were making a ruckus
Causing a fuckus
Preventing peace from having its way
So he stopped giving in
Stopped trying to win
Until those voices went away
Then he gathered his strength
And lunged towards the surface
To find what he already knew
That the difference between
Side A and side B
Is the difference between
Me and You

425.

There will never be enough time to say the things
That we don't know how to express

426.

My bones are changing
Melting
Shaping
Into who I was always meant to be
My heart is softening
Shining
Blazing
The world is opening up
For me
Who I was
And who I am
Are night and day,
A pearl and clam
My mind was chaotic
I've put it as ease
I conquered its labyrinth
Like a trapeze
My demons were fierce
Didn't want to submit
I sat with their darkness
Till it dissolved bit by bit
In the light of my Love
And the strength of my faith
In the frequency of harmony
My organs now bathe

427.

I know who I am
And I know why I'm here
To grab hold of fear
Pierce it with a spear
To trek through the jungles
Of darkness and fright
To capture our demons
And bring them to light
To stand for the powerless
The voiceless, alone
To speak for the children
To build them a throne
I'm here to make peace
On an island of chaos
After we release
All the old mucky moss
So, hide if you want
But it won't be for long
The Truth is emerging
I'm sounding the gong
We must look!
I declare
At our buried despair
We must feel
We must heal
To escape the Wheel
That has trapped us for eons
Our whole family line
We can no longer decline
It is now time to Shine

It is time to break free
To live in the Light
It is time to be brave
To gather our might
To peer deep within
And pick apart what we find
To overcome time
To transcend our mind

428.

I tried to be perfect
To not rock the boat
I held in my breath
So that I could float
I stuffed down my feelings
My truths and perceptions
I made myself small
To avoid rejection
I tried to blend in
Avoid the spotlight
I usually gave in
To avoid a fight
But another part of me raged
Provoked and instigated
In order to compensate
For my unexpressed hatred
It wanted to be heard
Acknowledged and seen
It needed me to stop
Assuming it was just mean
So, I let it come forth
I witnessed its fury
I allowed space to vent
Without any hurry
And I loved myself still
And I loved myself deeper
I found my true essence
And damn
She's a keeper

429.

Stop giving in
Stop letting them win
Those lower vibrations
They are not your kin
You carried them once
When you were all alone
But they cannot join you
Upon your throne
You must make your peace
Bid them ado
They can't come where you're going
You've got work to do

430.

Hi love bug
I'm here
I'm closer than near
I'm holding your hand
My sweet little dear
I regret my absence
My misguided allegiance
To your captors,
I identified with them
But I've left them behind
So that I could find
Your altar
And open the door
I'm here now
Forever
No longer a suppressor
I'm here to nurture you
To love you
To hold and to hug you
My dear one,
Little me
You are rescued and free
No longer bound
Not required to please
You are seen
You are heard

I just gave them the bird
You are safe
You are home
Shine your Light
Take your throne

431.

Take my hand
Through this storm
I will hold you
Keep you warm
Once it's over
You will find
We have left the past
Behind
No more drama
No more chaos
We'll be free of
All of their mess
It has never been ours
We were built for the stars
It is time now to see
We were born to break free
They will not understand
And that is okay
You don't owe them anything
You may go your own way

432.

Initiation complete
Personality accepted defeat
Soul has taken hold
Broken out of the mould
Divine union is at hand
It is time now to stand
In the Light of the Truth;
The essence of Youth

433.

I'm letting you go
Because you aren't real
My projections of you
Have finally healed
I no longer need you
To make me feel small
To consume all my power
To be your good doll
I'm free and I'm wild
I run like a child
I am golden and styled
No part of me mild
I laugh and I play
I frolic away
No longer beholden
No longer your prey

434.

This human form
Is a mess
It wants
It clings
It kneads
It stings
I am it
But it is not me
I love it though,
Through its eyes I see
Without this form
I could not be

435.

Trapped in a hall of mirrors
Make no mistake
What you see
Is what you are
No such thing as fate
Only choices
Day by day
Do something new
Or stay just the same

436.

The wall is crumbling
Brick by brick
The illusions are fading
The lies won't stick
Peering above
And what do I see
Naught but white doves
Harmony and peace
Those voices are gone
That internal chatter
The sun and the stillness
Are the only things that matter
I bask in the glow
Of my newfound foundation
Creator at last
Of a whole brand-new nation
A nation of peace
Understanding and love
Where justice roams free
Overseen from Above
The scales always balance
The night is the day
This land is our birthright
And we're well on our way

437.

Come with me
Past the glamours
And the notions of fate
Sail along on your ship
Through the little narrow gate
Leave your memories
And hopes
Your plans and desires
Bring your courage
Your flashlight
Your faith, and a smile
The Sea
She is rough
But she'll sure make you tough
You'll wash up on an island
Once you've finally had enough
You'll begin to come to terms
With the reality of yourself
You'll learn of your true nature
All alone with no one else
From there you'll sail again
Down a simple little channel
Thankful for the peace
And your trusty worn out flannel
And with contentment in your heart
And a smile on your face
The sun will shine upon you
You'll recognize the truth of this whole place

438.

Honeybees chase me home
Back to where I belong
I got caught in the web
Of a black widow's throne
I was blinded by sunlight
After years in a cave
I battled with Death
I conquered the grave
I was brought to new heights
On the wings of an Eagle
Then home to the Sea
By a friendly old Seagull
No longer afraid
No longer feeble
Eye open wide
And heart open too
I no longer look like me
Cuz now I am you

439.

You're a subtle instigator
A slithering snake
It's not your true nature
But the mask that you take
Imbued with the darkness
You hide and you crawl
Defending yourself at all costs,
You make others feel small
You lay and you wait
You pounce on your prey
Claiming the opposite-
That they just got in your way
Your fuse nonexistent
You could snap anytime
From happy to rageful
At the drop of a dime
You live in the shadows
Your dinner is hate
Breakfast is vengeance
Desert comes too late
I've been hunting you for years
Observing your predicament
Bewildered by your entitlement
Captivated by your belligerence
You are my father's face
Your mask is my inheritance
A good heart's fall from Grace
Shrouded in thick arrogance
Cuz it's not what you feel,
It is what you do

The facts of your behavior
Are what make you
You
So, I give up on your heart
You've chosen your path
I'm no longer your little girl
No longer afraid of your wrath
I still have compassion
For you, not your mask
But you'd never even know
Cuz your mask won't let you ask
I see your essence hidden
Though it's not the same as mine
I see the pain and heartache
Even though you say you're fine
I wish you'd stop pretending
Stop defending all your hate
Stop pretending this is normal
And rise above your fate
Remember who you were
Before your family crushed you
Find that little boy
And let His spirit come through

440.

I identified
With all the parts
That made me feel like home
Unbeknownst
All along
Their home was not my own
So I plucked them off
One by one
I set them free to roam
At last, alone
I discovered
My own heart is my home

441.

Pieces of you
Pieces of me
Who are these fragments
Of people we see
Where did they come from
And where do they go
Who do they belong to
Where is their home
Energies trapped
From a time long ago
Passed down the line
To put on a show
Spectacles of night
High and low vibrations
Fractals of the Light
Transcended by lustration
Our true essence trapped
In their funny hall of mirrors
Our inner child wrapped
Our heart kept in the freezer
Waiting for that great big thaw
Promised to our Earth
So let the glitters go
Prepare yourself for birth

442.

Men fall in love
With women who mirror
The image of feminine
They saw in their theater
Of childhood, that is
They way their mom loved them
That's from where their preferences
And fantasies all stem
But really what they're seeking
Is the essence of their soul
Woman is a portal
Into the greater Whole
It's why men give so much
To only be let down
No human could ever take the place
Of their own internal Crown
Men need to find the courage
To find their intuition
They need to give it a voice
And trust it beyond reason
Only then will we see
Men who can love fully
From a place of inner strength
And outward humble purity

443.

You left me for dead
Said it was all in my head
You all heard my cries
And kept telling me lies
My needs were ignored
My heart was abused
My essence dishonored
My purity used
I was not seen
Portrayed to be mean
A heart full of gold
Mined and then sold
I was chewed up
And spit on
Battered and broken
Humiliated
Laughed at
Kept as a token
You all had your way
Up until this day
Where I stand for my Self
And go my own way
I leave with forgiveness
For myself and for you
I've learned now what self-hate
And worthlessness can do
I couldn't speak then
But now have a voice
I used to be trapped
But now have a choice

I refuse to grow cold
Bitter or old
I'm reclaiming my confidence
My essence is bold
I'm proud to be me
I'm worthy of love
I know who I am
I am one with Above

444.

All of this time
I've been waiting on you
To make me feel loved,
To prove that it's true
What I could not see
Or properly grasp
Goes beyond the fact
That that wasn't your task
The love that I've needed
I learned to shut out
To keep my hands in a fist
My face in a pout
I kept my shell hard
My defenses strong
Which ironically kept out
What I needed all along
I needed to receive
But only learned how to give
Receiving had been dangerous
It always came with a tinge
Giving kept me safe
It made sure I was useful
Never mind the outcome-
Codependent and fearful
So I'm learning to be still
Open and receptive
Warm and soft and light
And to my needs attentive
I'm learning what it means
To be a woman fully

Now that I've gotten rid of
Those angry inner bullies
I'm learning to move slowly
To simply flow with life
I'm learning to be peaceful
To cut my ties with strife
I'm learning who I am now
Behind those worn-out masks
I'm learning how to live
Without that pocket flask
And crutches of dependence
And people-pleasing ways
I finally get to feel the Sun
And bask in his bright rays
My inner goddess healed
My masculine protecting
Our precious blooming field
Heaven is descending

445.

You tried to bring me down
Ten thousand ways
I fell down each time
More tired by the day
But I look at you now
And I see your despair
I see good intention
But a heart that's not there
I trusted you once
And that was my mistake
My internal worth
Was never yours to take
I look behind now
At the nightmare we were
No idea what we were doing
Never really sure
I'm stricken by reality
Brightly contrasted duality
Without my rose-tinted glasses
The whole show a depravity
You're still living in
That internal hell
But I can't help you now
You must escape your own well
You can keep your projections
Your shame and your blame
But I'm walking away
I am done with that game

I know who I am
And I know what I need
I know what I'm worth
I am finally freed

446.

Surprise!
Caught your face
Finally excavated you
From my space
You played your cards well
For a decade or two
Within your disguise
I never even knew
But my soul grew too big
My quarters too tight
I started purging out
The things that weren't right
Till at last came to you
My deepest protector
My ego, personality,
Identity defender
My own inner critic
Cunning deflector
Self-serving mimic
Straight up pretender
You've kept me confined
Insisting on safety
But you held on arcanely
Your motives unsaintly
Counteractive to freedom
To Heaven roaming free
But now that you're gone
I'm free to be me

447.

I learned what it means
To finally be seen
To be here and now
Placid and keen
To feel the wind blow
Through the veins of my blood
To sink to the depths
In the midst of a flood
To let it all be
Observe all that is
Finally at peace
At one with what is

448.

We're never alone
We are swimming in spirit
Perpetually surrounded
And that is the secret
Is it we who can't see
Who are too numb to feel
It is us who've decided
To block out the real
We are the ones
Who have chosen our guns
Defenses and barricades
Unscrupulous passions
We choose to ignore
What's in front of our face
We cling to the race
Disregard our saving grace
We spit on the graves
Of the ones who came before
Who are tapping our left shoulder...
Whispering there's more
We are blind to the Truth
We've plucked out our eyes
We rehearse our lies
Until this form dies
Then on to another
One more chance,
Mommy please
This time you go back
Don't ignore the bees
Sit with the trees

Observe their behavior
Be like the breeze
The whole world's in your favor
Open your heart
And set your mind free
Let the Sun be your guide
You have everything you need

449.

Inspiration struck me
Once I learned how to unstuck me
The Divine flowed through me
Once I learned how to undo me
To unravel my I
My definition of me
Once I learned what I saw
Is not what I see
Once I learned to let go
Open my window
Sit under the willow
Escape the bureau
To crack open my head
And pour out the Light
Once I gave up the fight
Stopped asserting my might
Yes the flow came right through me
Poured out between my eyes
There was no more time for lies
I had finally become wise

450.

I'm over the passion
I'm searching for peace
I long for stability
A presence of ease
I'm cutting anyone out
Who doesn't fit this bill
Who considers me last
After the egos they fill
I deserve a companion
That matches my heart
Someone I can count on
To trust from the start
I'm done with the games
I'm over the chaos
I've begun a new book
I'm sorry for your loss

451.

I don't know what to think
I don't know what to feel
In-between worlds
In search of what's real
In search of stability
Solid ground to stand
Fighting like hell
To escape this quicksand
It keeps pulling me back
But I'll never give in
Too focused on the win
To sink back into sin
And selfless self-betrayal
And unsuspecting doubt
There's no more room for clout
I'm vying to get out
So that I can get back in
Back to where I did begin
Inside this simple life
Just with a different spin

452.

I want to escape
But have nowhere to go
The walls are closing in
How low is too low
How much hurt could be left
To arise from that spring
What have I not felt
Buried under my wing
I'm so tired of this
I want to go home
I want to curl up
But don't want to be alone
I'm lost and confused
Don't know which way is up
The sadness so heavy
I just want to throw up
I'm weighed so far down
I can hardly lift my head
And now I can feel it;
The oncoming dread
The stab of abandonment
The sting of betrayal
My mind feels chaotic
My heart feels unstable
When will this end
Please
I've had enough
I knew it'd be hard

But never this tough
Please
Set me free
I have good intentions
I've served enough time
In this deep dark detention
Please
Let me go
My heart yearns to grow
To dance and to sing
To break from this ring

453.

I don't trust you
I don't trust me
I don't really trust
Anything that I see
Let alone what I feel
I've been stuck on this wheel
For so long I forgot
What is actually real
I'm ready to heal
But I just don't know how
I'm ready to run
But I've fractured my plow
My compass got busted
My sights gone adrift
I'm back to the puzzle
Through which I must sift

454.

Goodbye
And thank you
I'll see you in
Another life
You helped me heal
Showed me what's real
Brought to light
My inner strife
You broke my heart
A million times
Provided fuel
For a million rhymes
I let you go
Our last farewell
Through the furnace
Out of hell
I rise in flames
Shiny new
No longer the woman
You once thought you knew

455.

No one likes pain
But pain creates Art
Suffering provides
An impetus to start
To move, to evolve
To try something new
I don't like to stay stuck,
I don't know about you
So, let's embrace chaos
Destruction and fright
We need it to point us
Towards the things that are right
Towards the things that we want
What we need and desire
Let your pain be your compass
Let it fuel that inner fire
Let us welcome the ugly
The broken and raw
Let's throw away our band aids
And let our wounds thaw
Let's clean out the cobwebs
Put bulbs in the attic
Let's rewire our minds
And clear out the static
Let's look at it all
And decide what should stay
Rather than be drug
In any which way

Ignorance is useless
In a time such as this
But we each have our choice;
Ignorance or bliss

456.

Fungus grows
In the cracks
Turtles swim
On their backs
Robins nest
Underground
Honeybees swarm
All around
Oak trees dance
In the rain
Seedlings sprout
Yet again
Up is down
Into night
Buried deep
To find the Light

457.

Where is my playfulness
My childlike glee
I feel it in me
But others can't see
It's hidden somewhere
Or I should say she
She used to have fun
She used to be free
I locked her away
I'm not quite sure when
I learned being open
Was akin to sin
And equal to pain
And searing betrayal
The world was too harsh
And far too unstable
People like me
Didn't get to have fun
We were always rained in
Hidden from the sun
But I looked out the window
One dark dreary day
And spotted a woman
Who was unafraid to play
She was laughing and skipping
Dancing with delight
I swelled up with rage
I wanted to fight
I hated that woman
Yet I wasn't sure why

It turns out deep down
I just needed to cry
To dance in the rain
Until it renewed me
To feel all the shame
That had till then consumed me
I needed to feel safe
In myself and the world
I needed to reclaim
My internal twirl
To be there for me
To let myself dance
So, thank you, dear woman
For that one fateful glance

458.

The truth lies before me
It begs me to look
I'm lost in a dream
Like a fish on a hook
Surrounded by mirrors
And flashes of light
Something holds reality
Just out of my sight
I'm sleepwalking
Dream-talking
None of this real
It's all an illusion
We come here to feel

459.

Look
Over there
The veil is wearing thin
Look
Close your eyes
Let your true journey begin

460.

Are you who
You say you are
Or are you just
Another star
Buried deep
Way out of sight
Climbing slowly
Towards the Light

461.

How did we get here
And where shall we go
If we don't take that plunge
We never will know
But we must do it different
This time, not the same
We must be concerned
With our work
Not our name
With our goals
And our mission
With humanity at large
It must be our higher self
Who's in charge
No more bickering
No more fear
Just two hearts that are clear
Just a vision
Laid before
Shall we walk through
This door?

462.

If I haven't made it clear
I don't live in
The fear
I did
For a time
Before I learned
How to rhyme
To express
To reveal
What it is
I truly feel
Before I learned
About love
Before I saw
That white dove
Before I noticed
The rhythms
And patterns
Of life
Before I learned
To be still
To put away
The sharp knife
I lived in the fear
Because the fear
Lived in me
It had to be excavated
Before I could see
That my life
It was fine

It was perfect, in fact
It was beautiful
And blissful
Just a step past
The act
The role that I took
Just to keep myself safe
But my whole world was shook
Once I broke my failsafe
Once it all began to crumble
The illusion I'd built
Once I painfully saw
My reality on stilts
Shattered in pieces
To make room for the new
Then mushed up like dough
To rebuild
Something True

463.

A Fire burns inside of me
It rages on
No one can see
It is not rage of glum or fright
But rage of Courage,
Justice, Might
It burns for Truth
Ablaze for Peace
It spreads until
The lies do cease
It spares no feelings
Holds no shame
Its purpose righteous,
Not to blame
I am its keeper,
Container of Light
I temper It with
Unparalleled sight
Unwavering focus
Dedication to Love
I follow orders
From Above
I wield this Fire
For a cause
I work alone
Without applause

464.

What is this shit
The garbage in my head
Why do I feel
Like I'd be better off dead
When does it end
This circus called life
I'm feeling quite low
Keep me away
From the knives
How did I get here
And why did I come
I try to be happy
But still end up glum
All I thought that I wanted
I don't want anymore
I'm trying to find
A key to that door
The door to my passion
My hunger for life
I'm trying to find a reason
To put up with this strife
I don't know what I want
I don't know what I need
Right now, I hate everything
And everyone that I see
I guess that means I hate me
I don't care
I'm too tired
If I were my boss
I would make sure I'm fired

In fact
I just quit
I am done with this shit
I give up on life
The end
And that's it

465.

I'll see it when I believe it

466.

You stole my reality
Substituted your own
I was just a little girl
I never could have known
How dark it really was
Cuz you wouldn't let me see
You ignored the fights and screaming
Pretended all was glee
You made sure I stayed quiet
With the threat of withholding your love
You acted like you were a God
Heaven sent from up Above
You were just a fragile human
Too afraid to let me see
The ugliness of your demons
So they took hold inside of me
But I've come to set them free
To set the record straight
To traverse this twisted labyrinth
And expel all this self-hate
To find the Truth that lies
In the sparkle of my eyes
To excavate the lies
Try Reality on for a size

467.

I hide away
Tuck out of sight
I work by candlelight
The shadows call
Whisper my name
They lull me in the night
I yearn for Sun
And furthermore
It is my own birthright
I've learned to dance
Between the two
So they no longer fight
I rose above
The me vs. you
A balanced internal height
I merge the lines
Of good and bad
It takes all of my might

468.

You don't respect me
You never have
You take and take
And grab and grab
You steal my light
To feed your own
I was deceived
I should have known
I gave and gave
It all for what
To be left in the cold
All alone in a hut
The way you cut
So cunningly
You deceptively
Turn it all onto me
The perfect scapegoat
To hold your blame
To shoulder your burdens
To assume your shame
But I've had enough
I am not a trash bin
I am a white lotus
I do not accept your sin
This story's old
Covered in mold
My dawn is breaking
It's a sight to behold

469.

It's time to love me
Yes
It is
This responsibility
Is mine
Not his
It's time for a long bubble bath
Some background jazz
Belly of laughs
It's time for friends
And salads, too
It's time to dance
Long overdue
It's time to touch me
Hold me tight
To tilt my head
And face the light
It's time to remember
How it feels in December
When it's snowing outside
And I melt by the embers
It's time to cave in
And to let my love win
To let it surround me
To bloom from within

470.

Write
I must
In addition
To trust
No more lust
No more fear
No more muddled mind
Unclear
I am here
I am now
I'm about to find out how
The world turns in my favor
When I learn just how to savor
My delicious inner pudding
Once I finally find my footing
Once I love me back together
Once I finally untether
From the people places things
That have clipped my stunning wings
Once I sidestep those trappings
And surround myself with Kings

471.

I can feel you here
Within me
You write my words
So simply
I let you flow
You raise me up
You make me feel so whimsy
I'm a puppet
On strings
Those aren't strings
They are wings!
At your service
My master
Not to be mistaken for
A pastor
You are me
But I'm not you
Or am I
Who'da knew
Together we make three
Together I can see
The fragments left behind
And piece them with my mind
You whisper your secrets
You animate my face
You spur brand new moments
Right my story with Grace
Alas
You are my love
Swooped right in me

From Above
Inner sanctum
Treasure chest
A few cuts
Above the rest
Now I'm finally
At my best

472.

Who told me I was weak
Convinced me I was ugly
Who forced me to be meek
Bribed me to be grumpy
I can sense my power rising
The lies have melt away
Confidence surprising
Justice getting her Way
Up springs a brand-new day
A brand new me
A brand-new play
This one is quite enticing
Adventurous
And so exciting
I'll play my part
I wrote the script
Old story gone
Those pages ripped
I'm ready for
This brand-new start
Old reality
Crumbling apart

473.

I will not give in
I will not let you win
I will not put on
Those shackles again
I choose freedom
I choose love
I keep my eyes on
That white dove
The illusions
May be strong
But I'll prove those
Critics wrong
I have everything I need
It all started with a seed
It's the final push to sprout
Thats what this turbulence is all about
One last hurdle
Yet to face
I will finish
This race with Grace
No more testing
No more combat
I have found my
Inner bobcat
Strong and stealthy
Laser focus
Graduating from
Hocus pocus

474.

Oh my God
I love adventure
It is no longer
Mere conjecture
I've been playing small
But what's to lose
The fun is that
I get to choose
I choose pure joy!
I'm scaling this cliff
The jig is up
I've caught a whiff
Of real life
The OG me
Who loves to run
That's it
I'm in

475.

The soundtrack's on repeat
An unordinary beat
Playing in the background
From the rusty passenger seat
Sounds and songs from long ago
Reminiscent of childhood flow
An old and worn-out record
Wishing to let go
Hoping to be reborn
Clinging to a vision
Fighting against itself
Willing its own revision
Superior to man himself
Stunning in conviction
The old is trudged up
It is sifted and mourned
Each memory plucked
Each grievance dehorned
Until all that's left is the new
And the bare-boned true essence
No more glitches to skew
No more outstanding penance
From the dust and the grit
Springs a fresh sprout anew
The record is clean
And these wings are brand new

476.

Attention
Roll call
I am here
For it all
I am present
Standing ready
Laser focus
Hands are steady
Patient
Awaiting direction
In the arms of
Divine protection
Pure affection
True devotion
Humble heart
No erosion
Call me up
I am ready
In this Heaven
Land of plenty
Eros falls
Arrows deadly
I am armed
Glare is deathly
No mistakes
Standing still
No man can move me
From this hill

Till my God
Calls me forth
Compass facing
Only North

477.

Follow me
Into the dark
I hold all the keys
Invented the Ark
I want to be frank
And you to be brave
I'll sink in my teeth
Straight to the grave
Once I'm released
You won't have to wallow
The inside of your chest
Will stop feeling so hollow
Let me be free
And I'll run far away
You'll never look back
And never forget the day

478.

What
What is it
I'm here
I showed up
There
Take a look
Just inside of that cup
What's it say?
RSP
I just want you to move
Underneath
All this hair
Seems I'd not lost my groove

479.

My strict inner parent
You make danger apparent
Always searching for a threat
And alas
Threat, you get
You are drawing right towards you
The things that abhor you
And holding me hostage
Assuming I adore you
Let us out of this cage
Grab the key
Set us free
I don't need your protection
So go on your way

480.

The time has come
The time is now
No more waiting
Ask me how

481.

Seething
Breathing
Down my spine
Soiled
Broiled
Reak of brine
Absolute disgust
Bitter despair
Vile and insidious
Getting nowhere
My bones you crushed
Spirit lain bare
Your time is up
Go back to your lair

482.

I hate you now and
I'll hate you forever
Despicable swine
Impossible tether
Heart like leather
Love like ice
You had your chance
I rolled the dice
You cut me deep
Sliced each vein
No bright sunshine
Always rain
Was it all in vain?
You followed my family
Bearing your name
Feels like insanity
How can I unstick you
Finally get rid of you
What is a woman to do
But accept that I am you

483.

I want you to die
I want you to be gone
I've been trapped with your face
In my head all along
Perhaps I did choose this
And so what if I did
I choose something new now
I won't hear your bid
For my attention
My love and my time
I've reclaimed my devotion
Tuned to a new chime
The only way out
I've surmised with surprise
Is to relinquish identity
Fascination with time
To reach the sublime!
I must be my Self
With a capital S
Not a store-bought ego
From a shelf
We can work hand in hand
I suppose
And we must
But I will call the shots
Won't give in to your lust
You're filled with rust
And I love you still
And I love you in spite of
And I love you until

Forever runs out
Cus I don't know how to count
It's me and you baby
We're on a new route
With me by your side
You'll discover why they lied
You'll see your true colors
And the demons that try to hide
And the light that hides the deepest
Way down where it's steepest
Heavily protected
From the dark that tries to eat it
It cannot be lost
It can only be claimed
You are not broken
You have only been maimed
See beyond the games
The illusions
The facade
Let your Self be propped up
Filled with music
Filled with awe
Let us work together
Let us anchor Love
Let's move past this friction
Cuz we fit just like a glove

484.

Wow!
Whales
Dolphins
Mountains
What am I sensing
What is
Sensing me?
Are they the same
Are there things I can't see?
What's in a name
What's in an identity
What is an angel
Are you an entity?
Filled with empathy!
I am
Though it is not my own
It's only my experience
Through this vessel I've honed
In tune with the Truth
With a capital T
Not a scrap of facade
Through it all I can see
And little by little
Like a trusty old chisel
I chip and I pick
Till the gold I can lick
The Truth I can taste it
I can feel it
Inside
It finds me

Cuz I seek it
There is nowhere
It can hide
It lives inside!
Boy
What a ride
This life has been
I'll pass the Truth
To my Kin
So they can escape
This land of sin

485.

Underneath my hate
Is hurt
Behind the shiny glass
Is dirt
Why does it hurt
To let this go
Is it because
It's all I've known
You've treated me bad
But I still see your pain
I take on your hurt
I do all this in vain
I never deserved
You to treat me that way
But I still hope and pray
At the end of each day
I still hope and pray
That your heart will recover
I still hope and pray
That you'll come out from under
That dark hole in your head
And you'll learn how to love
And you'll love yourself first
That you'll forgive your past
And stop dwelling on the worst
I absorbed your pain
Like a sopping sponge
I didn't know how to look
Before taking that plunge
And I carry it still

And I long to put it down
But it hurts me to send it
Back to where it belongs
Cuz it never belonged to you
Or your parent's true selves
So where did it come from
And where is the valve
How do I relinquish
This burdensome load
It's keeping me trapped here
On this dark dusty road

486.

I'm laying down my sword
I don't need it anymore
This stance has gotten heavy
And besides
My back is sore
What was I protecting
But buckets of hurt and pain
It's time to stop perfecting
My mechanisms to block out the shame
It makes more sense
To let it go
To lay down the armor
To bathe in the snow
I don't want to cling
I want to sprout wings
I don't want to sting
I just want to sing
Goodbye
Heavy past
Goodbye
Useless blame
Hello
Fresh December
Hello
Bright blue flame

487.

You treat me like shit
And you don't give a shit
I don't throw a fit
Cuz I don't want to get hit
Or abandoned
Or hurt
So I eat my self-worth
I bury my feelings
Just to sit at your hearth
But your fire is out
It has never been lit
I've been searching for warmth
Someplace cozy to sit
It is time I pack up
And stop holding my breath
It is time to face the music
And look forward to what's next

488.

I'm beginning to see
The truth about me
And the love I've neglected all along
I'm starting to hear
Those whispers in my ear
Guiding me to where I belong
I'm sinking in deeper
To the open space beneath her
The womb that holds both dark and light
Embracing my true colors
Forgiving my past lovers
Finally giving up that futile fight
The Earth was right
All along
And she is right where
I belong
She lives in me
And I in her
I'm bathing in her
Assuasive myrrh

489.

Let's not pretend
That everything's all right
Let's not ignore
Your baby crying all night
Let's not assume
That parents always know best
In fact, let's just put that
Whole dogma to rest
Your indifference is cruel
"Cry it out" is abuse
Your baby's cry means they need you
What the hell is so obtuse?
Let's bring back common sense
And learn to parent from the heart
Let's be there in the ways
We should have been there from the start

490.

Sacred feminine
We bow before you now
We've trampled your sanctum
Crumpled your crown
You've been
Degraded
Violated
Dilapidated
Humiliated
You've been used and abused
Misunderstood and accused
And the time has come
To right our wrongs
To let you rise
Where you belong
The time is now
To set you free
To bow our heads
To bend our knee
To let you in
And let you out
To let you moan
And let you shout
To rid ourselves
Of heavy chains
To beg your forgiveness
And welcome your grace

491.

The more I let go
The higher I rise
Is it any surprise
To be born with new eyes
I didn't realize
How deep were the lies
Woven into the fabric
A parallel guise
Ideas and stories
Fabricated worries
Eating at our minds
Like worms out in quarries
It's all in our heads
The torment and dread
It'd be no less real
If any of us were dead
Cuz there's no such thing
As death
Just one life
To the next
Your form will change
The great exchange
To go learn something new
But you're still
You
You'll always be
And always have been
Just another
Me

492.

The tips of my roots
Keep reaching new depths
The most ugly
And vile things you can imagine
They're spreading out wide
Touching all sides
Of the darkest things
To be examined
And the highest of leaves
On the branches of me
Are singing of the glories Divine
Both sides grow in tandem
None of this is random
All of me
And Life
Is entwined

493.

My head feels so heavy
And yet seems so empty
Like what I think
Matters
Not at all
And the heavier it gets
The more I regret
Letting it put up
That thick wall
Between head and heart
It's been building from the start
Trying to protect me
From me
But I'm chipping away
Each and every day
To tear down that wall
So I can see

494.

Why am I striving
What can I not see
Is there anyone out there
Or is it
Just me
Why am I laughing
And crying and fighting
What did I come here
To be
And does any of it matter
When reality gets shattered
It all seems so silly
And cute
To run around pretending
There's no inevitable ending
It kind of makes the whole thing
Seem moot

495.

I did once
Try to fly
Before I lost my
Other eye
I got so high
But fell so hard
My body broken
Imagination charred
But a spark lived on
In the embers of me
It took many years
Before I again began to see
My hopes and my dreams
My desire to fly
To conquer my fears
This time touch the sky
And here I am now
Preparing for flight
Legs a bit shaky
Unwavering sight
To go or to stay
To let fear get in the way
To trust or to cling
To close my eyes
And swing

496.

I'm alone now
More than ever
What's this feeling
What's this texture
A glob of glue
Not yet hardened
Running amok
Sprinkled with garland
Nowhere to go
Not looking great
Questioning my destiny
Confused about fate
Am I late?
Why am I here?
How can I provide for
The ones I hold dear
I've been strung along
By the big guy upstairs
Consistently let down
Sinking into despair
It's not fair
Why me
What about the others
Why can't they see
Where is my glee
The Love I was promised
I'm searching in vain
If I'm being honest
I'm wandering the desert
Been thirsty for years

I've fought all the demons
I've faced all my fears
But still
I am here
All alone
In the dark
I'm losing all hope
Of ever finding
That ark

497.

It's so hard to sit still
I hate being me
When I sit here in silence
I hate the things that I see
My skin gets so itchy
My eyes start to well
Without my distractions
I am living in Hell

498.

I am no guru
Just because
I can see through you
The things that I see
Are extensions of me
I have mastered the art of
Owning what I see
And naming what I feel
And loving
What I hate
I have wrestled with the brambles
Way beyond that narrow gate
And I've been stuck
And I'm stuck now
And still I trust
Don't ask me how

499.

10 bare fingers
Chewed right to the bone
I hardly bat an eye now
When I hear my thumbnails groan
Leave me alone!
They shout
They despise being eaten
No doubt
But I'm all out
Of snacks
And toys
Of TV
And boys
I'm alone here
With me
Floating in this
Empty Sea
Or is the sky
The Sea
And my eye
In me?
I don't know
Hardly care
Shot my bearings
Lost my flair
Brittle hair
Chalky skin
Can't remember
How to begin

500.

How long can I run
I am under
The gun
Scurrying so that
I can't see
The life that I've built
The stage that I've set
The drama playing out
Starring
Me

501.

Trust
Fall in line
I am all out of
Time
It's too late to put my faith in
Things I see
Plunge
Take that dive
To finally feel
Alive
I'll take one
For the team
But don't thank me

502.

Does my face hold my secrets
Can you see them written there
Can you see past my sweet smile
Down deep to my despair
Can you hear my darkness cawing
Feel my essence crawling
Can you sense my demons dancing
See my angels prancing
What do you see
When you look at me
A woman
A girl
Did you catch a glimpse of
My pearl
Do you feel a light
An impulse to
Take flight
Run away from
My sight
How about an urge
To fight
What is right?
Who's to say
I should make you feel any
Certain way
Just take note of
What arises
Let it show you
Your own surprises

503.

I used to run
All the time
Before I learned
How to rhyme
I ran from the Truth
I ran from the pain
Ran from discomfort
Ran from the rain
Nearly went insane
Nearly ran out of fuel
Everywhere I ran to
Held another duel
I hated school
And I hated real life
Each edge was a torture
A sharp scorching knife
I preferred to stay safe
Comfortably numb
I wanted control
Others under my thumb
But I became sick
I had outgrown my cage
My hamster wheel busted
Curtains went up on stage
Suddenly
All my rage
Was in front of my face
Suddenly
Sitting still
Had taken running's place

An Ace
From above
Forced me
To Love
And my only choice
Was to sit
To face the hurts
To take the hits
And my only option
Was to grow
To heal and
Let go
To trust and
To receive
The Ace hidden
Up my own sleeve

504.

Deep down inside
My loneliness resides
Beneath layers of addiction
And a faulty sense of pride
A small black empty void
A defective aneuploid
Hungry for a wholeness
At the very least a closeness
Something to assuage
This bitter bleak aloneness
In search of utter rapture
A remedy for this fracture
The split within my psyche
That makes me think I might be
Borderline insane
Unnervingly arcane
Blatantly profane
Alas
I can explain
But why
Try
Could it be that I
Am a lost cause
Full of useless hope
I've been hanging for years
At the end of my rope
And there's nothing but time
To wait and consider
Why the harshness of life
Has not made me bitter

The audacity of my dreams
To others might seem
Like a method to cope
Superior to dope
But I
Must try
Otherwise
I should die
I'm determined to fly
Find my wings
Touch the sky

505.

What's it gonna take
For me
To love me
To enjoy my own company
Be my own cup of tea
Could I like me
For me
No distractions
No phone
Could I be my own friend
Happy being
Alone
Could I make myself moan
And light up with laughter
Could I bathe in delight
And not tell anyone after
Could I tell myself secrets
Make my own inside jokes
Enjoy a solo dinner
Cook up some artichokes
It's my only hope
Cus I'm
All I have
And I should be grateful
And I should be glad
That at least I am nuanced
Though slightly off kilter
It's fun to be lucid
To get rid of my filter
I think I'll learn to love me

And be there for myself
It seems infinitely wiser
Than depending on anyone else

506.

It was magical thinking
To believe that you were choosing
The damage you were doing
Afterall
You're only human
Sure you cared about me
But that was not enough
You should have faced the truths of you
And dealt with all your stuff
At the very least
I should have been taught
That none of this treatment
Was ever my fault
Instead we went on pretending
That all this was normal
We kept on defending
Our story we all held so dear
Of a small happy family
Borne out of fear
We lived in a castle of lies
I learned to be blind
To not trust my own eyes
And then I built the same for myself
A small wobbly family
That looked good on a shelf
But inside it was rotting with pain
With fighting and outbursts
With confusion and shame
Until finally I spotted the pattern
Thanks to my suffering

And a big thanks to Saturn
I could no longer live in that paradigm
I ran out of patience
I ran out of time
I gave up on the illusions I'd built
And I tore down the family
That was standing on stilts
And I stood for the first time
For me
And I took my sweet time
Teaching myself how to see
And it took all the courage I've got
To shatter the illusion
For so hard I'd fought
But finally
At least
I was free
And I built a foundation
Dependent
On me

507.

I was living in delusion
Trapped in an illusion
Replaying childhood
Till I looked under the hood
And what I found
It caused me to shudder
I was paralyzed with fear
Developed a stutter
But I refused to give up on my light
I needed to see
With unfiltered sight
What was the point of this fight
And it took all my might
To not make myself right
But instead search for what I had missed
Under the umbrella of love
The magic of a kiss
And finally
I have come to this
Love can't be confined
In confinement we miss
The Truth about just who we are
Our infinite nature
Our place in the stars
And romance
It builds us a cage
It keeps us performing
Up there on stage
So we must have the courage to look
Deep in ourselves

Not inside of a book
And see what we came here to be
Joyful and glistening
Wild and free

508.

I had to reclaim my focus
From the people places things
That were feeding on my empathy
Sitting on my wings
I had to divert my attention
Into a whole new direction
Crank up the solitude
To increase my magnitude
I've now earned my fortitude
And I'm filled with gratitude
A whole brand-new attitude
And amplified latitude

509.

Is it any wonder
When our life roars with thunder
After sitting on our power
For one too many hours
It's easy to flop
To limp and to gimp
To whine and complain
About all of the rain
But it's better to rise
Let our flame reach the skies
To harness our energy
Transform our inner chi
To build something new
With the blocks of the old
Dream a new vision
Create a new mold
To remember our sovereignty
Stop living in poverty
Recognize our novelty
And tend to it constantly
It is time to become
Who we've been all along
To throw away the script
And sing our own song
To shoot for the stars
That live deep inside
And throw away the crutches
Upon which we've relied

510.

The thrills and the falls
I am here
For it all
The heartache and pain
It is never in vain
The sunshine and bliss
The love in a kiss
The turbulence and flair
The entropy and despair
I am here for the highs
And I savor the lows
And I walk in the middle
Cuz I know where this goes
I acknowledge the fury
I am not in a hurry
I embrace every droplet
Sit still in each flurry
I am one with this life
I nuzzle her bosom
As she whispers her secrets
And I beautifully blossom

511.

Wholeheartedly
Unguardedly
Unabashedly
Impartially
Skillfully
Artfully
Gracefully
Honestly
I
Love

512.

My love for you
Held depths with no bounds
I could see to your soul
Interpret your sounds
There was nothing you could say
No thing you could do
That I did not justify
Because I knew you
Because I knew who you were
Behind all the masks
Because I saw all your pain
And your burdens and tasks
You never had to ask
It always just was
I never had a reason
I loved you because
In the center of your eyes
I saw more than a man
I saw infinite galaxies
I saw my life's plan
And as I clung to this Love
It forced me to surrender
Every facet of me
That kept it undercover
It broke me wide open
Again and again
And I kept coming back
I could never say when
Because when never comes
In the Light of pure Love

It's a never-ending gift
That comes from Above
But reality hit
Only once I did see
I wasn't looking at you
I was looking at me
Then this Love
It exploded
Erupted from within
And finally
At last
I was permitted to begin
My true Work on this plane
As loyal defender
Of the Light inside each of us
I became its reflector

513.

As I sit
And consider
Why pain makes some bitter
And makes others rise and take flight
I am struck with the notion
There's no magic potion
Just eyes that are starving for sight
And hearts that are desperate for Truth
And minds that are willing to sit
Cuz to fly
Is our right
It requires no might
It asks only that we
Embrace it

514.

How many years
Must slide on by
Before we notice
That hole in the sky
That portal to something much deeper
That small blinding light
Beckoning us to seek her
What will it take for us to stop
To sit still and listen
To what we've been missin'
And just how much pain is enough
To exit the parade
And quit being tough
When will we notice the clues
The signs and the symbols
Begging us to choose
To wake from our deep, dreadful slumber
To answer that call
Live life in full color
When will we stand for our Selves
Claim our Divinity
Find peace in simplicity
And when will that point be for You...
To call your own bluff
And find what is True

515.

What a miracle
To Be
Alive
To be One with what Is
The Sea and the Sky
I marvel at yet another day
To be in this skin
To witness this play

516.

Shhhh
Take a breath
Just sit still
And listen
Shhhhh
Close your eyes
You came on
A mission
Wake up
Sweet child
Remember who you are
Surprise
Moon child
Your heart is
A Star

517.

I fell out of my car
And rolled down a hill
Covered in mud,
I met a man named Bill
He laughed at my predicament
Exclaimed it was magnificent
To see another escape
The old rat race
He warmed me up some dinner
Told me the truth about sinners
Then handed me a map
I couldn't read
He warned me it'd be lonely
And for a while, smoky
But one day I'd be glad for all this mess
Then he walked away and vanished
For a while I felt banished
Until I came upon a trusty squirrel
Who shared with me his treasures
Gave me extra for good measure
As I learned to sink into the whirl
I was scared and I was shaken
I feared I was forsaken
Until the washing machine
Spit me out to dry
I was sparkly and clean
No longer sad and mean
Then I saw Bill again
On the other side

518.

Don't you just love
A story about Love
A happy ending
Pulls right at those strings
But this story
Is about us
In love with what's Above
Just waiting for us
To leap
And find our wings

519.

All around me
People walk
No idea where they're going
Or why
All around me
People talk
No idea that they're heard
By the sky
No idea that they hold all the power
To change their life
Within an hour
No idea that they hold all the keys
No idea they are one with the trees
Confused and in pain
Avoiding the rain
That they need to water their seed
Convinced of their name
Searching for fame
Too blind to see they have everything
They need

520.

Hear me!
See me!
Feel me!
Know me!
I am a budding flower
I'm reaching for the Sun
I've braved the dark
And murky soil
Now it's time for fun
It's time to express
To be uniquely me
To relish the experience
I was sent down here to see
It's time now to sprout
There's no need to doubt
Being our Selves
Is what Life's about

521.

One in a million
That's what they say
One in a million
Will make it to
The Way
And I write for You,
True Seeker
To guide your journey
Deeper
I've felt around these walls enough
I found the switch
I turned it on
Now I can see
And so can you
Once you stop
Feeding what's not True

522.

Don't talk down to me
I am not beneath you
Don't walk out on me
Don't you know that I need you
Don't shun me
Or hush me
When I'm learning
Don't rush me
I'm your child
Give me love
Give me cuddles
Give me hugs
You don't own me
Don't control me
Make me laugh
Don't leave me lonely
You're my guide
For better or worse
Don't leave me empty
Quench my thirst
Be my friend
Be on my side
When I'm mad
Don't run and hide
Let me feel
And let me shout
Let me cry
And let me pout
Hold my hand
When things get tough

Don't walk away
Say you've had enough
For me It's rough!
I'm so confused
The world is scary
I feel abused
I need compassion
I need your heart
I need encouragement
To become Art

523.

This time is about me
I'm learning what I like
I'm learning what I love
I'm learning what is right
People-pleasing was so ingrained
I never even saw it
I thought that I was selfish
How horribly ironic
I put others first
To relieve my own responsibility
Never once grasping
The sad and sheer futility
Cuz I only met takers
They didn't know how to give
But it was only my fault
I was too afraid to live
Too afraid to find my voice
Too afraid of my own power
Too afraid that if I learned to take
I would be treated sour
But all this changed
Around the time
I learned to love myself
To hear my heart
And put her first
Before everyone else
My compass fixed
No longer cracked

Became my trusty guide
It showed me
All the things I want
But always tried to hide

524.

From the top of the world
To under a stump
This coaster is old
I despise this lump
That lives in my chest
Down under my breast
Always threatening to enlarge
Remind me who's in charge
Always ready to take
My own hard-earned peace
And replace it with fear
I must cut its lease
I must cut my ties
And allegiance to intensity
The extremes have grown old
And I've lost my propensity
To traverse high and low
At such rapid rates
My Soul years for stillness
A reprieve through pearl gates
The storm can rage on
But I
Must stand still
Committed to Peace
I would die on this hill

525.

When does it end
When can I say
That I made it
When can I rest
Take a break from the mayhem
Can I let down my guard now
Stop obsessing over just how
I'll be hurt yet again
Let down in the end
Can I reverse this tick
That keeps me stuck flinched
Expecting a hit
I'm so tired of being split
I just want to trust
Want to shake off this rust
So I can run jump and play
No matter what others say
When does
The fun come back
Without
The heart attacks
When can I flow
In love and
In Know
My shoulders are heavy
From this self-imposed levy
But whom do I owe

Am I free to go?
It don't feel that way
I feel shackled and gray
Trapped in a prison
God said I was risen

526.

Empty promises
Blatant lies
Anger wrapped in
Sweet surmise
Misplaced outbursts
Raging flight
Who is wrong here
What is right
What is real
And what came first
Should I stay concealed or
Will I burst
I'm out of time
I'm done with hoping
These bitter drinks
Don't help with coping
The past is here
It laughs in my face
Masquerading as my future
An ugly disgrace
I will not choose either
But then I'm still right here
Fighting the present
Avoiding my fears
I crawl into a ball
And out my eyes I bawl
Succumbing to hopelessness

Feeling so small
No drive to walk down that hall
Towards more disappointment
So I'll sit still and shatter
Until my anointment

527.

Unable to speak
About what I am feeling
Unable to think
My mind is stuck reeling
Forced to ignore
What's in front of my face
Forced to accept
A blatant disgrace
Persuaded to smile
In a situation so vile
Conned into confusion
Bamboozled by guile
Cut off from access
To my own inner truth
Replaying the scenes
From an unresolved youth

528.

Is it the people around me
That are keeping me stuck
Or is it just my
Own internal muck
Are they not just reflections,
Projections of me?
Are they not here to show me
Where I am not free?
It's so easy to blame them
But it's just a distraction
I must look much deeper
At my own inaction
My own love of comfort
And reliance on others
Perhaps it is I who
Loves suckling on udders
Perhaps I'm afraid of
Claiming my life
Maybe that's why I settled
For being a wife
Under the knife
And under the gun
The clock ticks right by
I've hardly begun
To lace up my bootstraps
And be on my way
I was waiting for another
But must pave my own way

529.

It took a long time to see
That the dark side of me
Was not to be shunned
Or feared or abandoned
It needed my love,
Understanding, compassion
The dark kept me safe
It shielded my light
It defended my life
When I was too young to fight
And I owed it respect
And I owed it my time
I owed it expression
And it came out in rhymes
And it's part of me now
And it lives on my face
As a message to others
Who are lost in this place
And I stand for the dark
Just as much as the light
None of it's wrong
Because all of it's right
And I gave up the fight
And I opened to both
And I became whole
And pledged both an oath
To hear both sides out
On every occasion
And to understand each
Without identification

530.

Within the chambers of my heart
I harness pain
And make it Art
I see it with
My Knowing eye
I let it breathe
I let it cry
I let it go
To be transformed
And it comes back bright
And it comes back warm
I do this daily
Bit by bit
This is my work
I cannot quit
Till the pain is gone
And my Soul takes flight
And I see the world
From a whole new height

531.

I know who I am
And where I belong
I know being free
Means singing my own song
I know now what it means
To be a human fully
Overcome by Spirit
Who overcame my inner bully
The bridge to the past
Was the key to my future
And the silence within-
The remedy for my stupor

532.

This anger ran so deeply
I was sure it can't be mine
My own disowned inheritance
From my father's line
It burns me up so strongly
My bones are searing hot
I want to punch a fucking wall
But that might hurt a lot
How do I channel this
What do I do
I don't want to hurt me
I don't want to hurt you
I sense there's a freedom
Attached to this Fire
But I'm scared to
Let it run free
I think that I'll use it
To defend the child
That lives inside of you
And in me

533.

I knew my purpose
From a young age
And it was to be free
To break out of my cage
To access my rage
And to use it to fuel
A new way of thought
A new type of school
To defend the weak,
Innocent and abused
To give them a voice
With passion infused
To shine a bright light
On the ways we are harming
Our sons and our daughters
The reality's alarming
I was gifted a sensitivity
So acute it's a curse
Each tear a syringe
But things could be worse
I use this to feel
Painfully deep to the real
To the way your kid feels
About things you think are no big deal
Oh
How excruciating it feels
To be a kid in this world
To take your abuse
All the garbage you hurl
Each word like a knife

Every dark thought a hammer
I can feel every ache
Behind your harsh mindless banter
Only now can I see
The full purpose of me
And the life I had to live
To become Who I must be

534.

I'm tired of thinking
Exhausted, in fact
I'm done with this role
Over this act
This story is old
And I'm growing more bold
Ready to launch
Right out of this mold

535.

All the money in the world
And for what
Who does it help
If I sit on my butt
And cater to me
And ensure my needs met
I yearn to help others
Whom I have not met yet
I yearn to speak Truth
To share the wisdom of health
I've learned giving it away
Is the secret to Wealth
I've learned it's not about me
And it never has been
I'm a piece of a puzzle
When I'm me
We all win
When I found my true Self
And I shared it with ease
I no longer felt lost
No longer diseased
When I stopped chasing money
And instead, chased my joy
I became rich
I became the real McCoy

536.

You've never been there
You've never been around
When I needed you the most
You were nowhere to be found
I needed a foundation
Not flittering flirtation
You had no real vocation
All you offered was frustration
You're a useless jerk
A lazy bum
Go stroke your beard
Drink some more rum
You're being evicted
From your place in my head
You make my world ugly
You're better off dead

537.

At the root of my being
Sits a crumbling mess
More anger and heartache
Than I care to express
I was born into chaos,
Confusion and pain
But I cling to the hope
That it wasn't in vain
I've never felt safe
Never once been secure
Whenever I got comfortable
Disaster would occur
But now it's time
For me to build
With solid stones and bricks
After clearing away
My inheritance
Of broken glass and sticks

538.

What is a man?
A real one, I mean
I'm afraid I've never known
He has yet to be seen
But as I heal myself
And my own inner masculine
I anticipate devotion
Dedication and discipline
I anticipate integrity
And strength of character
I look forward to humility
A heart that really cares
An openness to life
Adherence to strong principles
A loyalty so fierce
It makes me feel invincible
And as I nurture these qualities
Within my very own Soul
It is the law that outwardly
We will go on a stroll

539.

One of these days
My work will pay off
The days and nights
I've spent alone
Teaching myself how to love
The buckets of tears
Dissection of hurts
The painful acceptance
Of all of my warts
The decisions I've made
Towards the life that I want
And the courage to leave
The people that haunt
This time of reflection
Has been a real feat
But it couldn't be different
I couldn't accept defeat
I could not live a life
That was not my own
Pulled around by forces
From the unknown
And now I can say
As I stand here today
That this life is mine
And I've built it this way

540.

We're all at different levels
Protected by angels
Fighting off devils
We all see the world through a lens
It scuffs up our view
It's in need of a cleanse
We all share the very same essence
And individual Souls,
In need of our presence
And we all could use some more compassion
From ourselves and from others
And way less distraction
In fact there's so much that we share
Yet we fight over nonsense
Like styles of hair
If we just could look past what we see
We would see we are One
I am you and you are me

541.

There's nothing new
Under the Sun
It all has been said
It all has been done
But I've never seen from this view
I've never been me
And you've never been you
And that's what we come here to see
A brand-new perspective
Once a fly
Once a tree
Finally human
At last
We can write our own cast
Create our own story
No matter how gory
It's all by design and by plan
We fritter into fragments
Take form as a clan
And play with ourselves in this way
So take a deep breath
And let yourself smile
Before you know it, you'll be on to
A new play

542.

I'm home
I'm safe
I'm right where I belong
The world around
Still looks the same
Won't be that way for long
Cuz inside, I've shifted
Through all the pain I've sifted
I left behind the memories
And found my inner treasury
I saw a warm light
Embracing and flowing
Calling me towards it
Yellow and glowing
It was stable and safe
Strong and secure
It was honest and humble
Beautiful and pure
I took a deep breath
Before I closed my eyes
I let go of the past
Let go of all the lies
I let my child curl
In the arms of this strong Light
I set my feminine free
Finally let go of the fight
Between these sides of me
And the barrier between
The reality of life
And what I'd made it mean

543.

What is this lull
This void in my skull
Hijacking my sight
Portraying life dull
What am I missing
Still cannot see
Is someone holding me back
Or am I doing this to me
I just want to breathe
Want to lay down and rest
I've given this my all
My absolute best
So maybe I'll stop trying
Just relax and I'll find
The simple Truth of life
Behind the harsh grind
Of time
And effort
And thinking non-stop
I've been carrying this load
But it's time for it to drop
I've taken it on
But it's never been mine
Without all this weight
I'll harmonize
My Trine

544.

Blessed Garden
Cornucopia of my mind
Watered from the roots
Driven up from the ground
Evolving decade to decade
Engaging in my terrain
Developing complexity
Finding simplicity
Refrain to refrain

545.

Ok now
Here I am
About to leap
At the brim
Letting go
Into flow
I look outside
I see the snow
I look within
I see the Sun
I sense my journey's
Just begun
I love you, mind
You're not my master
With you subdued
We rise much faster
What are we after
Nothing at all
We're letting go
Allowing the fall
Into the bliss
Of what really is
Into this moment
Into this

546.

When I try to find you
You disappear
When I close my eyes you're
Always there
When I try to
Figure you out
I am left with
Confusion and doubt
When I silence my mind
The answers appear
The Truth becomes obvious
Reality clear
But when I try to
Pin it down
I'm empty handed
Like a clown

547.

Inching closer
Day by day
Towards the Light
The One True Way
Falling often
Still, I rise
Longing for those
Brand new eyes
Tearing off my
Old disguise
Sifting quickly
Through the lies
Making friends with
All the voices
Meticulously crafting
All my choices
Letting go and
Letting in
Pure surrender
Let Love win

548.

I'm teaching me how to
Be gentle with me
Acknowledge my feelings
And let them all be
I'm hugging myself
And stroking my face
Embracing my spirit
My own inner grace
Enjoying this place
And all it entails
Even those moments
I fly off the rails
It's all for a purpose
The spiral keeps spinning
Making its way
Back to the beginning
With wisdom in stride
And chaos under wraps
I start again fresh
With a pocket of snacks
This time prepared
Eyes open wide
No more confusion
I'm here for the ride

549.

My inner masculine
Was worked to the bone
Clinging tighly
To his throne
He kept a brave face
But inside was crying
Working so hard
But dreamed about dying
I kept him suspended
Made him perform
Never any breaks
His clothes were all worn
He kept me protected
But at a steep price
He needed my love
Which was frozen like ice
I emerged from my dungeon
And brought him some cocoa
I had conquered our demons
Was no longer loco
I let him relax
Put him at ease
We were finally healed
No longer diseased
I offered him warmth
Brought him in from the cold
And he offered me safety
And a strong hand to hold

550.

Here I am again
Confused
Thought I was being loved
But still, just being used
And abused
And taken for granted
I'm over all your lies
And seeds of doubt you planted
In my inner garden
You stomp around in boots
Every time I plant more love
You dig up all the roots
You're in cahoots
With Satan
To bury all my light
You make my life a living hell
It's constantly a fight
You always must be right
God forbid you're wrong
You'll make believe that you know best
And you've known all along
I'm done playing along!
I'm over this whole drama
Maybe you'd know how to love
If you ever had a mama

551.

One part of me loves fighting
Another part is meek
One part's keen on hiding
Another loves to seek
One part feeds me scraps
Another reminds me I'm full
One part says I'm weak
Another knows that's bull
Who's right? Who's wrong?
And who's to say
It matters much at all
I'm all these things
And none
The real me
Laughs at it all

552.

I take in the gush
The mush and the goo
I turn it to fun
To light and to fuel
I breathe in the hate
I exhale pure love
This is my gift
It comes from Above

553.

Afterall,
It's not you
That is taking from me
It's my own loss of self
My own irresponsibility
It's my own lack of boundaries
Of not knowing how to take
It's my deep ingrained masks
It's my Self being fake

554.

I am you
And you are me
Just close your eyes
So you can see
How can this be?
How can it not
We're all made of the same
It requires no thought

555.

Moving the chaos
Letting it rain
Washing my body
Keeping me sane
If I keep it inside
It'll fester and sprout
So it moves through my body
Till it finds a new route
And I pour it in artwork
And I pin it to paper
Afterall, it is formless
Not even a vapor
And my job is to mold it
To harness its power
My role is to use it
Before it turns sour
Let the world see your chaos
Let the Sun see your pain
Your life is your canvas
It is never in vain

556.

I find myself here
Surrounded by villains
They look like my family
But they're really just fill-ins
Fragments of me
Just waiting for me to see
That I'm really not them
Because I am me
I was born into darkness
To bring it to Light
Surrounded by wrongs
To make them all right
And now it is clear
To escape from the fear
All I need is to trust me
And remember why I'm here

557.

Anyone can do it
Anyone can be
A person of strong character
Living in integrity
Hold yourself accountable
To what you really want
Tear apart your masks
Let go of the front
Don't rest upon your laurels
But strive for deeper truth
There's nothing left but time
To discover the obtuse
When the drinking gets old
And you're left out in the cold
Surrounded by your demons
You must let the light take hold
Don't wait until your old
To let this battle rage
Face your fears courageously
And escape your liminal cage

558.

Underneath the surface
I'm digging with a razor
Searching with a microscope
Looking with a laser
I've picked apart the old
So I can build the new
I've sliced my tethers free
No longer bound by you
The past is dead and gone
I'm waiting for the dawn
I'm waiting for the sound
Of my own victory song

559.

The ultimate gaslight
The family disease
Pretending it's normal
Painting me diseased
You hurl your projections
I have no protections
I stand still and take it
My toughness
I fake it
It hurts
I can't lie
I'm alone in this maze
Trying to see clearly
But everything's a haze
Who am I
In all of this
I thought that I knew
Is there something I missed?
I know that I'm not
Who you say that I am
I'm the black family sheep
The sacrificial lamb

560.

Sinking despair
Deep
Deep
Deep
Pain
Trying to protect them
All of it in vain
No longer can ignore
I don't fit in with my past
No longer trying to change it
Or trying to make it last
I'm over the drama
I'm done with the fighting
There's nothing here to salvage
I need a change of lighting
There's just so much that's riding
On the choices I make now
I need to make the right ones
I'm trying to learn how
To stand still in my Soul
Despite the outer chaos
To grab hold of the Truth
And rise above the pathos

561.

It's not love
It never was
Who could see this coming
No one ever does
We carry our ties
To the pains of our past
And repeat them again
Expecting it to last
And it takes time to see
What we really ought to be
And it takes time to be
Untangled up and free
And by then it's too late
The damage is done
The kids have been born
No one's having fun
And at that point
You realize
That the world has fed you lies
That every single person
Is just you in disguise
So the way to receive love
Is the same way that you give it
Only this time,
Pour it inward
Anywhere else
And you'll regret it

562.

Thank you
For this opportunity
To heal
To rise above the
Hamster wheel
It's been painful
Sheer disaster
But I couldn't have gotten here
Any faster
Without the mirror
Of your face
Without the pain of
Your embrace
I'd still be blinded
Clinging to illusion
Instead of nearing
Inner fusion
There's still confusion
I'll admit
But I'm becoming
Ok with it
I'm feeling whole
I'm feeling free
I'm over you
And in love with me

563.

The waves keep crashing
One by one
I fear this ride has
Just begun
I catch my breath and
Am pummeled once more
I can't find my bearings
Lost sight of the shore
How much more
How much more
How much more
Can I take
How much heartache and torment
Before I just break
Before I just shatter
And dissolve into space
I'm longing for rest
I'm desperate for peace
I'm holding my breath for
My promised new lease

564.

Finally
Finally
I love myself now
I knew that I'd get here
But I never knew how
I didn't know what it'd take
But I knew what was at stake
I needed to love me
For my own daughters' sake
I needed to show them
How to stand for themselves
How to have their own backs
Without depending on anyone else
It's important that they know
How to water their own Soul
It's imperative that they grasp
That they are both already whole
I had to stop engaging
With the things that held me down
I had to face my fears
I had to claim my Crown
I couldn't let them down
And now, one day they'll see
I did all this for them
Because they did all this
For me

565.

Why do I keep running
Where am I going
Why can't I sit
Embrace my own Knowing
Who holds the answers
Are they outside or in
Neglecting my Self
Is the only real sin
There's nothing to win
And there's nowhere to go
There's nothing to fix
Only new seeds to sew
So it's time to let go
Time to give up this fight
Time to open the shutters
Time to let in the Light

566.

I searched
And searched
Outside of me
I looked
And looked
Desperate to see
Desperate to understand
Desperate to Know
What the Hell was going on
What was the point of this show
And who I was
And why I was here
I read every book
I faced every fear
I asked every guru
I turned every stone
I forsook the world
Walked the mountain alone
My legs became weary
I was losing the fight
It wouldn't be long
Till I lost all my might
So I sat by a tree
And I threw in the towel
My mind was a mess
And my worn shoes smelt foul
I found myself worthy
For the effort I gave
And I found myself brave
For escaping those caves

And I closed my eyes gently
For the first time in ages
And I finally saw
What was not in those pages
I saw my own Soul
The True essence of Me
And I finally laughed
And so did the tree

567.

You cut me down
Then act like you didn't
I feel what you're doing
Though you say it isn't
Undercover
Manipulation
Stealing my power
Humiliation
Keep me under your thumb
Docile and numb
By thwarting my confidence
Do you think I'm so dumb?
You make me feel small
To make yourself large
Your condescending tone
Keeps you in charge
Cuz I'm just a kid
I'm desperate for acceptance
I need your approval
Not unending petulance
And I fell for it then
But I'm standing up now
I can't believe I
Let you rule me somehow
I'm reclaiming me
And my inner safety
I'm healing my masculine
Energy you dimmed

568.

I caught a glimpse
Just a glimmer
Of who I was
When I used to shimmer
I used to sparkle
I was silly and fun
Way back before
The nightmare begun
Way back before
I built all those walls
Way back before
I made myself small
Before I learned that
Love was cruel
Before every moment
Became a duel
I was trusting and hopeful
Sweet and secure
Eyes open wide
Not yet covered in wool
I guess that's what happens
Around the time you turn 8
Your whole world gets flipped
You enter a new gate
A portal to lessons
Your soul came to learn
An experience of the opposite
Of that which you yearn

So that you can rise
Overcome the guise
Trudge through all the lies
And reclaim your true eyes

569.

All I've ever done
Is run
All I've ever chased
Is fun
No wonder I could not
Feel the sun
I had to go back to
Where this begun
The running
And hiding
The sabotage
And lying
Which part of me
Was in charge of deciding
That it was unsafe
To be where I was
That I wasn't allowed
To be who I was
Why did I let them
Take my security
Why did I give them
My own damn authority
I've built a new space
And it's inside of me
A place where I'm loved
A place where I'm free
And I provide these things for me
No one can take them
My heart is my castle
My unbreakable sanctum

570.

I yelled at the sky
I was barren and dry
My God
He forsook me
When calamity strook me
I cried out for help
But help did not come
So I renounced all hope
For a time, became numb
Was I dumb?
Naive?
Following a lie?
Surely my God
Would not let me die?
But he would
I surmised
And to my surprise
A raging relief
Of tears struck my eyes
Once I let go
Of that God in the sky
I finally broke free
With my wings, I did fly
Cuz born on that day
In the pit of my core
Was unshakable faith
In my own inner roar
And at last

I discovered
God does not dwell outside
And as long as we look there
That long he will hide

571.

People pleasin'
Always cheesin'
Always lookin'
For a reason
To offer help
To be of service
Never peering
Below the surface
Never seeing
How much you take
You give to feel needed
Not for goodness' sake
You don't give from love
You give from self-lack
This backwards game
Is kind of whack
I don't want your help
Don't need all those strings
I'll make my own way
I'll use my own wings

572.

Deep in my womb
I hold all the Light
There is no more fear
There is no more fright
I'm ready for flight
I'm ready to be
Colorful with glee
Wild and free
I'm sinking down deeper
Left the mind behind
Down into rhythms
The Earth left me to find
I'm feeling my pulse
It is one with creation
I'm leaving the old
Crumbly foundation
No speculation
Cuz I can feel it
I sense what's coming
I'm drawing near it
I hold the keys
I know the answers
I'm joining ranks with
Life's real dancers

573.

I entered a cave
Dug out deep within me
I followed a light
It was dim
Hard to see
I stopped for a rest
Then I crawled through thick sludge
I was quite lost and weary
But my body wouldn't budge
I emerged
On a cliff
And a wizard scooped me up
He put me on his shoulders
And offered me a cup
Up there, I saw the World
The real one
I had won
Everyone was laughing
Playing
Having fun
He tore away my limits
And my hands turned to balloons
I drifted up
Until down there
They all looked like cartoons
I saw the clouds
And all the land
Yet still inside myself
Who knew
Within

Existed things
Like continental shelves
I caught a glimpse
Of some crocs
They were circling
A dock
And I was headed
Right down towards them
My body
Started to lock
And he grabbed me
Wizard man
And took me back to
Happy land
And he warned me
To be careful
In a free world such as this
Cuz all the fears inside of us
Are impossible to miss
And if we've not yet honed our minds
To let in what we want
We're sure to see
The underside
Of all the things that haunt

574.

Words are useless
How ironic

575.

Who are you
Without your mask
Society tells us
Not to ask
We cake them on
Day by day
When we go to work
Even when we play
We fake that smile
Always polite
Underneath we
Want to bite
We've lost our fight
We've lost our power
They slip right off us
In the shower
Till we rise up
Rip off these faces
Righly claim our
Proper places
Till we stop defending
This thing called I
And learn to see with
Our other eye
Till we take a stand
A stand for Truth
And start sorting through the lies
That started at our first lost tooth

576.

Knock knock
Open up
Let my pure gold
Fill your cup
Don't hold back
Don't shut down
Let's get off this
Merry go round
Let life flow
And let love win
We'll start this whole show
Over again
Piece by piece and
Brick by brick
Let it crumble
Be the wick
Be the Soul
That stands in spite of
All the pain that
Really might've
Crushed you dead
Taken your head
But you let it go
Graduated from red
And now it's time
To rise up, new
Into this moment
No more blue

Only white
Radiant Light
You've earned your wings
Now take flight

577.

Does it matter if I
Make a sound
Can anyone hear me
Underground
I'm crying out
I'm all alone
Seething rage
In every moan
Where have you gone, God
Why aren't you here
Left me for dead
Trapped me in fear
Just make it stop
The sleepless nights
The constant pulling
The fruitless fights
I'm only human
I need a break
I don't know how much more
I could possibly take
For fuck shits sake!
I'm dead
Depleted
I fucking hate you
And this soul you seeded

578.

A manipulative
Whore
An unwanted bore
An arrogant prick
Always greedy for more
Who are these masks
Who owns these faces
They open up doors
To unwanted places
They climb in our windows
When we're too weak to fight
They make us feel safe
They make us feel Right
But who are we, really
At the least
None of these
They hijack our systems
They're nothing but theives
They are not us
But we pretend we are them
If we step back a notch
We can reclaim our helm
If we look
Through young eyes
We'll see past our
Own disguise
We'll remember where
We learned the lies
And try our Soul on
For a size

We'll reclaim our
Innocence
And our wholeness
Without mince

579.

I don't know what love is
But I know what it ain't
I'm not seeking perfection
Not expecting a Saint
But I'm looking for real
And I'm looking for raw
And I'm longing for a safe place
For my cold heart to thaw
And I found it
In me
In who I came here
To be
I created a place
Deep inside where I'm free
And I'm safe and I'm home
And my hearts free to roam
And I can run fearlessly
Right into the unknown
Cuz I've trudged through the depths
And I've scaled to the heights
And I've faced all my fears
Overcome all my frights
And I've learned that I'm stable
And I'm sturdy and warm
And I've learned that the real me
Has been here all along
And I buried her deep
But her light knew no bounds
And I answered her call
Following her soft sounds

And she beckoned me home
Right to true Love's embrace
And now
In the mirror
I can see her soft face

580.

Seeking and seeking
And looking and looking
The heat is turned up
I can feel my mind cooking
It does not want to die
To relinquish its grip
It's gasping for air
It's fighting that whip
The whip of my Soul
As it nudges me forward
Blinding my eyes
Forcing me inward
The pain feels so real
But it's all self-inflicted
It hurts to change patterns
So deeply imprinted
My Soul does not hurt
It knows only Love
It reminds me that this
Is a gift from Above
And as my mind screeches
And it grasps and it moans
I sink even deeper
Into the unknown
And I find my soft center
My valley of peace
And the reckoning stops
And time begins to cease

581.

I'm here to be soft
To be open and brave
I'm here to rise up
Born anew from the grave
I'm here to take off
Every mask ever known
I'm here to build up
My own Heavenly throne
Not for me
Not for you
But for all of us
At large
I'm here to remind you
Who's really in charge
And I'm here to pay homage
To that glimmer in your eye
And to lift your chin gently
Towards that one in the sky
I'm here as a servant
And my master is Truth
I'm here to display
The pure Light of Youth
And I'm here to uncover
All the beautiful darkness
To show to the world
That it's actually harmless
And to befriend it all
To blow up that thick wall
Between head and heart
So we can all learn to crawl

582.

Out of my cage
Out of my shell
Out of my self-imposed
Version of hell
Trapped and betrayed
And deeply unworthy
Lo and behold
Afterall
I am worthy
I am worthy of Love
Of laughter and peace
I am worthy of Life
And a whole brand new lease
On it
Here I sit
No more deficit
I've taken the reigns
And transformed all of it
All along
I've been whole
All along
I've been free
All along
My perspective
Has been up to me
And I've chosen the fear
But not anymore
I am breaking that lease
I have walked out the door
No more

No more
No more
I am home
I belong
Free to write
A new song
Free to be me
Free to see
Reality
Past all the
Illusions
That buffer
And filter
And cause dark
Contusions
And I brought in
The Light
No more reason
To fight
No more need to
Take flight
I am one with
The Night

583.

I was looking
For me
Although I could not see
Distracted
By you
And the things I thought I knew
Blinded
By darkness
Pierced by
The starkness
I reached and I lunged
And I grasped and I clung
Tripping over myself
Nearly blowing
A lung
Alas
It'd begun
My search for the seeker
Hidden in plain sight
My own sacred keeper
I held all the keys
I only needed to look
Within my own heart
Instead of a book
And it hurt
To let go
Of everything I did know
And it hurt
To break free
Of every word said to me

But all lies
Deserve to crumble
And I could feel my
Belly rumble
With a hunger
For the Real
With desperation
To Feel
And to heal
And to roam
And to find my true home
And it's in me
Deep inside
Where I peacefully
Now reside

584.

My human is exhausted
She's tired and worn
She's contemplating life
Regretting being born
But I push her still
Because I know no other way
To break down her hard wall
And let me have my way
She must release her grip
She must give up control
She must forego her mask
She must stop playing a role

585.

My precious armor
I must bid you farewell
You've kept me so safe
But I'm starting to swell
I needed you once
But you no longer fit
Your rigidity is tight
It now hurts to sit
Your metal is strong
Protection so fierce
Nothing could touch me
Not even a pierce
No, I can't feel the pain
But, I can't feel the Love
I can't feel a thing
I've been comfortably numb
I need to break free
From your beautiful shell
Which once felt like home
But now feels like Hell
It's time to be brave
Face the highs and the lows
Experience the turbulence
Cuz God only knows
That the purpose of life
Is to feel it all flow
To live in the Now
To let all else go

586.

Afterall
There's only Love
Everything else
Is a lie;
A fumbling of reality
A blurry unclear sky
To be cleansed
From within
Is to wash ourselves
Of sin
To forego dark illusions
To call bluff on all exclusions
To remember who we are
And live from that soft place
Is impossible for man
Without amazing Grace
Without a lofty battle
Without an inborn Might
Without an old wise soul
Born ready for a fight
A fight within ourselves
A fight against the lies
A fight to let Love win,
To reclaim our sovereign Eyes
So begin before you're ready
I know your heart feels heavy
But only you can choose
To toss aside that levy

587.

I stopped trying
To do
To be
To get somewhere
To see
To escape myself
To accomplish more
To keep my sights
Upon that door
And I sat
And did nothing
I accepted
An inner something
A peace
A pause
Totality
Without cause
Without question
Without motive
I jumped off the
Locomotive
And I became
What I had sought
And I understood
What the masters taught
Full acceptance
Of what is
In the Now
It's all there is

588.

I thought that love was lust
So I gave myself away
In hopes that they would love me
In hopes that they would stay
In hopes that I would get the love
I needed from my father
In hopes that I would be approved
Instead of such a bother
I gave and gave
The best of me
They took and took
The rest of me
Tapped for juice
My precious Light
Giving in
Without a fight
Till one day
I said no more
I stood right up
Ripped out those cords
I breathed me in
I felt my power
Sweet release
Of all the sour
Standing tall
And bold and brave
Rising out of
That old cave

At one with life
In Union with me
Remembering now
Who I came here to be

589.

When I'm feeling down
And it happens a lot
I try to remember
Back to when I was taught
I was taught as a tot
That it was not ok
To pout or to shout
Or to have a bad day
I was taught as a tot
To silence the crying
To shove down the hurt
When I felt like dying
But I teach myself now
To sit in the rain
To feel every flurry,
Every brushstroke of pain
I let myself be
And I give myself space
And that's why I'm free,
Why I can see in this place
Cuz I'm on my own side
And I have my own back
Now nothing outside
Has need to attack
I've loved all my parts
And I've brought them all Home
And I set my Soul free
And together, we roam

590.

My inner spark
The essence of me
Was buried away
Where no one could see
But I've reclaimed it now
And I gave it full power
To captain our ship
To tear down that old tower
And it steers us with Love
And it burns so damn bright
And you have one, too
And it needs you to fight

591.

The very last step
The final boss
To face my fear...
My fear of loss
The sadness that arises
From being alone
The shame that emerges
When I'm all on my own
To stand tall alone
And to know I'm enough
To rely on Love
And to stop being tough
To take what I've learned
From 30 years in the dark
To share it with the world
To leave my True mark
To right all the wrongs
By realizing they were rites
To be a pure vessel
For a world that needs my Light

592.

I have nothing else to say
I'm done
I've said all that I could
I've come to terms
With the idea
Of being misunderstood
To those that find some resonance-
It's to your souls I write
I write to find my clarity
I write to see The Light
I forgive everyone everything
I have no grudge to bear
Life always works out perfectly
Everything is fair
The pain comes with a gift
The trials serve a purpose;
To crack our hearts wide open
So we may be of service
So take the leap
Unlock your past
And write your story new
So you can find
Which gift inside
The world has birthed in You

READ THE REVOLUTION

JOIN THE REVOLUTION

@realsamanthaminerva

CONTACT THE REVOLUTION

revolutionthebookseries@gmail.com

Made in the USA
Monee, IL
01 September 2025

23638889R00208